THE DIVINE *Virtues*

14 VALUES TO LIVE BY

RICHARD RIFE

CFI
Springville, Utah

ISBN 13: 978-1-59955-390-0

Published by CFI, an imprint of Cedar Fort, Inc., 2373 W. 700 S., Springville, UT 84663
Distributed by Cedar Fort, Inc. www.cedarfort.com

LIBRARY OF CONGRESS CATALOGING-IN-PUBLICATION DATA

Rife, Richard C. (Richard Carlos), 1953-
The divine virtues : 14 values to live by / Richard Rife.
p. cm.
ISBN 978-1-59955-390-0
1. Virtues. 2. Christian life--Mormon authors. 3. Church of Jesus Christ of Latter-day Saints--Doctrines. I. Title.
BX8656.R645 2010
241'.0493--dc22

2009049126

Cover design by Jen Boss
Cover design © 2010 by Lyle Mortimer
Edited and typeset by Heidi Doxey

Printed in Canada

10 9 8 7 6 5 4 3 2 1

Printed on acid-free paper

Dedicated to my dear wife, Janet, who inspires me to strive to be my best self and whose example and thoughtful comments have made this a much better book than I could have written on my own.

Acknowledgments

For some years now, the doctrine that we can acquire in our lives the divine virtues, thus eventually becoming like our Father in Heaven and His Son, Jesus Christ, has occupied my mind and pressed itself upon my feelings (see D&C 128:1). This book is a result of my studies on that subject and my halting attempts at self-improvement.

It's probably amusing to those close to me, who know my foibles and weaknesses, that I have written a book about becoming more Christlike, but they have had the courtesy and kindness not to make fun of me, at least to my face.

I am very grateful to my wife and best friend, Janet, for her support as I worked on this book. Even more importantly, I appreciate her consistent example; she was wonderful when I married her thirty-three years ago, and she just keeps getting better, which is the whole idea. Many of Janet's insights found their way into this book with or without attribution to her.

Thanks to my children and grandchildren for treating me with love and respect and for filling my life with joy. One reason for wanting to take upon ourselves the divine nature is so we can live eternally with our families. In my case, my family members are just the kind of people I want to live with eternally.

My sincere appreciation goes out to Cedar Fort for its willingness to publish this, my second book; to Heidi Doxey for her careful and effective editing of this book (and also for kindly saying she enjoyed reading the book and thought it was beautifully done); and to Jen Boss, who created a beautiful cover for my Christmas book, and who did it again for this one.

I am grateful to the people, living and dead, famous and not widely known, whom I have cited in the book as good examples of the divine virtues. Their examples have inspired me and have shown me that it's possible, in this life, to make much progress on the pathway to perfection.

Finally, I express my love and devotion to the two loving Beings who embody the divine nature. I know that it's worth it to continue striving to be like Them.

THE DIVINE *Virtues*

14 VALUES TO LIVE BY

Also by Richard Rife

Honoring Christmas in My Heart

Contents

Preface viii

1. The Divine Virtues 1
2. Humility and Meekness 7
3. Obedience and Submissiveness 19
4. Faith and Hope 31
5. Charity and Love 44
6. Patience and Long-suffering 55
7. Temperance 67
8. Diligence 77
9. Kindness and Gentleness 90
10. Easiness in Being Entreated 98
11. Holiness, Godliness, and Virtue 105
12. Knowledge 115
13. Mercy 129
14. Gratitude 140
15. Happiness 148
16. Conclusion 159

About the Author 166

Preface

THIS BOOK IS ABOUT ACQUIRING the divine virtues, or as the Apostle Peter called it, taking upon ourselves the "divine nature." There are several ways to describe this quest—to acquire the Christlike or Godlike attributes; to become more Christlike or Godlike; and to perfect oneself (or, at least, to make progress toward perfection).

You might think it takes a lot of nerve to write a book about becoming like God. What kind of person would undertake such an effort? I guess I would. But it's not because I think I'm perfect. It's because the scriptures and our prophets clearly teach us that taking upon ourselves the Christlike attributes is one of the main purposes of this life.

I don't think I'm a Christlike person, but I truly would like to become one. One of my heroes, President Spencer W. Kimball, thought it was permissible for an imperfect person to write about becoming Christlike. He said, "In writing about sin and repentance, no intent is implied that either the writer or any of those quoted, except the Lord himself, is without fault. But we would not have much motivation to righteousness if all speakers and writers postponed discussing and warning until they themselves were perfected!"[1] I am certainly not perfect, but I have decided not to postpone discussing the important subject of seeking the divine virtues.

In recent conference addresses, Elders Dallin H. Oaks and David A. Bednar have taught the importance of *becoming*, as opposed to just *doing*. Nothing could be more important than becoming more like our

Heavenly Father and His Son, Jesus Christ, for as the risen Lord Jesus told the Nephites, "What manner of men ought ye to be? Verily I say unto you, even as I am" (3 Nephi 27:27).

When the Apostle Peter encouraged us to become "partakers of the divine nature," he explained that some of the qualities of the divine nature are faith, virtue, knowledge, temperance, patience, godliness, brotherly kindness, and charity (see 2 Peter 1:4–7). My study of the Godlike qualities listed in this and other scriptures has led me to believe that they can be grouped as follows:

- Humility and meekness
- Obedience and submissiveness
- Faith and hope
- Charity and love
- Patience and long-suffering
- Temperance
- Diligence
- Kindness and gentleness
- Easiness in being entreated
- Virtue, holiness, and godliness
- Knowledge
- Mercy
- Gratitude
- Happiness

As you read this book, it will become obvious that these Christlike qualities are not separate or distinct. Just as ink on a page sometimes smears and bleeds over into other lines of type, the Godlike qualities bleed over into one another. For example, mercy is a manifestation of charity. Patience is akin to temperance. Submissiveness is obedience in its highest form. And humility is a prerequisite for faith and hope. One attribute is not mutually exclusive of another, nor is any one attribute self-contained. However, for the purposes of this book, I will separate them into these categories to aid in the discussion.

This book is not intended to be a lengthy treatise. Rather, it is intended to be inspirational, encouraging, and edifying. Perfection cannot be realized in this life, but with God's help and our effort, we can make substantial progress.

I hope you will enjoy reading this book. I hope it will inspire you—as writing it has inspired me—to make the pursuit of the divine virtues a major focus of your life.

Note

1. Spencer W. Kimball, *The Miracle of Forgiveness* (Salt Lake City: Bookcraft, 1969), xii.

1

The Divine Virtues

When men correctly understand and have faith in the true and living God, they strive to develop within themselves his virtues. He becomes the lodestar of their lives. To emulate him is their highest aspiration. As they strive to "be . . . perfect, even as [their] Father which is in heaven is perfect" (Matthew 5:48), they actually become partakers of his divine nature. In doing so, they add to their faith and knowledge, temperance, patience, godliness, brotherly kindness, love, and charity, virtues that are perfected in the true and living God. These virtues drive out of their hearts selfishness, greed, lust, hate, contentions, and war. Happiness, contentment, joy, and peace naturally follow.

—*Marion G. Romney*[1]

If you ask any Primary child why we are here on earth, he will answer, without hesitation, "To obtain a physical body and to be tried and tested." That's true. And isn't it wonderful that we have this knowledge at such an early age? But even more important than the Primary child's response is the fact that we are here on earth to become like our Heavenly Father. We have the seeds of divinity within us, and life's purpose is to cultivate those seeds.

Joseph Smith said, "If men do not comprehend the character of God, they do not comprehend themselves."[2] Because of the Restoration, we know who we are—and who we can become. President David

O. McKay taught that the mission of the Church is "to develop in men's lives the Christlike attributes."[3] He also wisely taught that "man's earthly existence is but a test as to whether he will concentrate his efforts, his mind, his soul upon things which contribute to the comfort and gratification of his physical instincts and passions, or whether he will make as his life's end and purpose the acquisition of spiritual qualities."[4]

As taught in the scriptures, and mentioned in the preface, those Christlike qualities, or divine virtues, are:

- Humility and meekness
- Obedience and submissiveness
- Faith and hope
- Charity and love
- Patience and long-suffering
- Temperance
- Diligence
- Kindness and gentleness
- Easiness in being entreated
- Virtue, holiness, and godliness
- Knowledge
- Mercy
- Gratitude
- Happiness

It may seem odd, but as we start our discussion of becoming like Jesus, I would like to quote a scripture that describes those who will inherit the terrestrial—not the celestial—kingdom: "These are they who are *not valiant in the testimony of Jesus*; wherefore, they obtain not the crown over the kingdom of our God" (D&C 76:79, emphasis added).

This scripture implies that to inherit the celestial kingdom, we must be valiant in the testimony of Jesus. In the April 2002 general conference, Elder Neal A. Maxwell explained how to do this: "The best way to *valiantly testify of Jesus* is to become steadily more like Him."[5] And, as Elder Maxwell wrote on another occasion, "Real adoration of Jesus as our Savior . . . will lead us to emulation of Him."[6]

How do we obtain the Christlike qualities? How do we emulate Him and become steadily more like Him? We can learn something from the attempts of Benjamin Franklin, a great early American inventor and diplomat. Franklin helped draft the Declaration of Independence and the U.S. Constitution. He was truly a great man, but also a flawed man, just like the rest of us.

Benjamin Franklin decided to acquire for himself thirteen virtues, which include some of the divine virtues we will discuss in this book. Franklin's thirteen virtues were temperance, silence, order, resolution, frugality, industry, sincerity, justice, moderation, cleanliness, tranquility, chastity, and humility.[7] He made a chart and systematically focused on each virtue for a week at a time, rotating through them every thirteen weeks. As he did this, he found that he did well on the virtue he was focusing on for that week, but not so well on the other qualities. In his old age, he concluded, "tho' [sic] I never arrived at the perfection I had been so ambitious of obtaining, but fell far short of it, yet I was, by the endeavor, a better and happier man than I otherwise should have been if I had not attempted it."[8]

What Benjamin Franklin may not have known is that developing the Christlike qualities is an interactive effort. We have to try our best, and we have to repent when we fail, as we undoubtedly will fail. When we do this, God then changes our hearts and helps us acquire the divine virtues. Over a long period of time, with our own effort and with God changing our hearts, little by little, line upon line, precept upon precept, grace for grace, we can gradually take upon ourselves the Christlike qualities.

The important thing is, we have to try. It is our life's purpose to become more like Jesus. It is not our life's purpose to:

- Become rich
- Have pleasure without responsibility
- Achieve fame or notoriety
- Obtain power, real or perceived
- Become a government or business leader
- Hold a high church calling

Jesus taught: "For what shall it profit a man, if he shall gain the whole world, and lose his own soul?" (Mark 8:36).

Benjamin Franklin tried to win the thirteen virtues through his own effort. It's true that our best efforts will be required and that we must repent along the way, but without the active participation of the

Lord, we will never be able to become like Him.

Ultimately, the Christlike qualities are given to men through the Atonement of Jesus Christ. It takes an interactive effort—a man doing his best to obtain the divine attributes, and God changing the man's nature so that he does indeed become more like Jesus. So we must try, and God will make up the difference over time.

Perhaps the most definitive Christlike quality is charity. From the Book of Mormon, we learn a very important point about how charity, and perhaps the other attributes, are obtained. "Wherefore, my beloved brethren, pray unto the Father with all the energy of heart, that ye may be filled with this love, which he hath bestowed upon all who are true followers of his Son, Jesus Christ" (Moroni 7:48). Charity is bestowed upon us. Although we must do our part to obtain it, charity is a spiritual gift.

In the remaining chapters of this book, we will explore the attributes of Christ, His divine virtues. As you read, you may find that you have already made substantial progress on some of the virtues. Perhaps you are naturally humble—I wish I were—and arrogance has never been a problem for you. However, you will undoubtedly find that you are falling short on some of the other attributes—I know I am. I hope you will be encouraged to focus where your focus is needed, make your best effort, and ask God for His help. This book is intended to be encouraging and edifying, not discouraging. There is hope for all of us—in fact, hope is one of the Christlike attributes.

We have many examples to follow as we strive to take upon ourselves the divine virtues. Our ultimate example is Jesus Christ, and in each chapter we will look at how His life exemplified the divine virtue being discussed. But there are also mere mortal examples we can look to: prophets, saintly sisters, exemplary parents, local church leaders, and true friends. President Spencer W. Kimball was a great example to me when I was a young man. His humility, diligence, and charity clearly reflected the characteristics of the Lord, whom he served so spectacularly. My dear parents, though they were both born and raised in a mining town and probably had a more expansive vocabulary than other Utah County Saints, nearly perfected the traits of charity and brotherly kindness and were among the most cheerful and happy people I have ever known. The bishop of my youth, William J. Pratt, was a kind, loving, cheerful, and life-changing Church leader. I have also known many sisters who are amazing examples of the Christlike attributes, and I have been blessed to serve with many men who are holy and devoted servants of the Lord.

None of these mere mortals was, is, or can be perfect in this life. But many of them are godly individuals who have taken upon themselves the divine virtues in large measure.

Gospel scholars Joseph Fielding McConkie and Robert Millet wrote about the importance of good examples. "As a child learns by imitating and emulating parents and those older than himself, so we learn godliness by imitating others who have set an example in righteousness, especially Jesus Christ. Alma appropriately describes this process of becoming Christlike as receiving the image of Christ in our countenances."[9]

Consistent with what Brothers Millet and McConkie said, in my journey to become more Christlike, I have greatly benefited by emulating the positive examples of my leaders, parents, and other friends and associates.

Jesus said, "Therefore I would that ye should be perfect even as I, or your Father who is in heaven is perfect" (3 Nephi 12:48). He would not have said this had He not meant it. Nor would He have said it if it were not possible. I have no illusions about the difficulty of this quest. I know it will be a long road. Much effort, prayer, repentance, time, and soul-wrenching will be required. But, oh, what a great adventure it will be!

Summary

- One of the main purposes of this life is to learn to be more Christlike, to acquire the divine virtues. The purpose of the Church is to help its members become more Godlike.
- Celestial persons are those who are valiant in the testimony of Christ. The best way to valiantly testify of Jesus is to become steadily more like Him.
- Developing the Christlike virtues is an interactive effort—we try our best and God changes our hearts over time, making up the difference.
- The life of Jesus Christ offers the best example of the divine virtues. However, we will also benefit by emulating the positive attributes

of Christlike individuals, such as Church leaders, parents, friends, and other associates, even though these wonderful individuals are not perfect in this life.

- Jesus said, "Be ye therefore perfect," and He meant it. It may be a long road, but it is possible with God's help.

Notes

1. Marion G. Romney in Conference Report, April 1970, 67.
2. Joseph Smith, *Teachings of the Prophet Joseph Smith*, comp. Joseph Fielding Smith (Salt Lake City: Deseret Book, 1976), 343.
3. David O. McKay in Conference Report, April 1941, 106.
4. David O. McKay, *Steppingstones to an Abundant Life* (Salt Lake City: Deseret Book, 1971), 28–29.
5. Neal A. Maxwell, "Consecrate Thy Performance," *Ensign*, May 2002, 36, emphasis added.
6. Neal A. Maxwell, "Jesus, the Perfect Mentor," *Ensign*, Feb. 2001, 8.
7. Benjamin Franklin, *The Autobiography of Benjamin Franklin*, ed. Frank Woodworth Pine (New York: Henry Holt and Company, 1916), 147–49; accessed online via Google books.
8. Ibid., 158.
9. Joseph Fielding McConkie and Robert L. Millett, *Doctrinal Commentary on the Book of Mormon*, vol. 3 (Salt Lake City: Bookcraft, 1991), 30.

2

Humility and Meekness

In reality, there is, perhaps, no one of our natural passions so hard to subdue as pride. Disguise it, struggle with it, beat it down, stifle it, mortify it as much as one pleases, it is still alive, and will every now and then peep out and show itself; you will see it, perhaps, often in this history; for, even if I could conceive that I had completely overcome it, I should probably be proud of my humility.

—*Benjamin Franklin*[1]

We begin our study of the divine virtues with humility and meekness. We start with humility because it is the foundational attribute. If we are not humble (or at least trying to be humble), we will never gain the rest of the attributes. We won't even want to try.

While serving as a mission president in Korea, I prayed for experiences that would help me become more humble. Almost immediately, and for a full month, I had a number of excruciatingly difficult experiences, all of which caused me to feel more humble. It got so bad, however, that I went back to the Lord in prayer and said it might not be a good idea to make me humble so quickly.

Maybe I didn't want to do it so quickly, but it is true that learning to be humble is a key purpose of this life. Elder Bruce R. McConkie taught:

> In a sense, Jesus here [in Luke 14:11] summarizes the whole plan and purpose of this mortal probation. It is to test men and see whether they will seek for worldly things—wealth, learning, honors, power—or whether they will flee from pride, humble themselves before God, and walk before him with an eye single to his glory. Without this basic Christian virtue of humility there is neither spiritual progression here nor eternal life hereafter. With it men are able to gain every godly attribute in this life and to qualify for full salvation in the mansions on high.[2]

Without humility, it is impossible to obtain the other Christlike attributes. Elder Alexander B. Morrison, emeritus member of the Seventy, wrote, "Is there, then, one single attribute of character that best characterizes the man or woman of Christ, enabling him or her to subdue the 'natural man?' Some might say love, courage, faithfulness, or integrity. Without in any way decrying the importance of each of the above, and many others as well, I submit that perhaps the most Christlike of all attributes of character is that of meekness, or in other words, humble submissiveness."[3]

Example of Jesus Christ

Jesus said, "Take my yoke upon you, and learn of me; for I am meek and lowly in heart" (Matthew 11:29). If He is meek and lowly in heart, then we, His followers, must be meek and lowly in heart as well.

In His earthly experience, the Lord truly was meek and lowly in heart. Creator of the universe, He condescended from His throne on high to live here upon the earth as one of us. He was born in a manger and walked the dusty streets of Palestine. He lived humbly and experienced the vicissitudes of life. In performing the Atonement for us, He descended below all things, suffering punishment for all sin, guilt, infirmities, and weaknesses, somehow fully comprehending mortality so He could comfort and succor us (see Alma 7:11–12). Although the greatest of God's spirit children—the Only Begotten Son—He humbled himself and put His Father's will before all else. On His path to the cross, He was ridiculed, spat upon, questioned, hit, stripped of His clothing, whipped, and forced to wear a mock crown. And yet He bore it all in silence. What humility, what meekness, what submissiveness! He even said, "Father forgive them" (Luke 23:34). Truly He is the greatest example of the divine virtue of humility.

The Apostle Paul wrote aptly of Jesus' humility: "Let this mind be in you, which was also in Christ Jesus: Who, being in the form of God, thought it not robbery to be equal with God: But made himself of no reputation, and took upon him the form of a servant, and was made in the likeness of men: And being found in fashion as a man, he humbled himself, and became obedient unto death, even the death of the cross" (Philippians 2:5–8).

When I think of Jesus taking "upon him the form of a servant," I see Him in my mind's eye washing His disciples' feet, showing and teaching us what it means to be a servant-leader:

> [Jesus] riseth from supper, and laid aside his garments; and took a towel, and girded himself. After that he poureth water into a bason, and began to wash the disciples' feet, and to wipe them with the towel wherewith he was girded.
>
> So after he had washed their feet, and had taken his garments, and was set down again, he said unto them, Know ye what I have done to you? Ye call me Master and Lord: and ye say well; for so I am. If I then, your Lord and Master, have washed your feet; ye also ought to wash one another's feet. For I have given you an example, that ye should do as I have done to you. Verily, verily, I say unto you, The servant is not greater than his lord; neither he that is sent greater than he that sent him. If ye know these things, happy are ye if ye do them. (John 13:4–5; 12–17)

Jesus truly humbled Himself and came to earth in the form of a servant.

The Sacrifice Required of Us

It is important for us to follow Jesus' example by humbling ourselves. In this context, it is good to consider the sacrifice God asks of us. In Old Testament times, the Lord required His people to perform animal sacrifices. However, under the new covenant, a different sacrifice is required. The Savior explained to the Nephites what we are now required to sacrifice:

> And ye shall offer up unto me no more the shedding of blood;

> yea, your sacrifices and your burnt offerings shall be done away, for I will accept none of your sacrifices and your burnt offerings. And ye shall offer for a sacrifice unto me a broken heart and a contrite spirit. *And whoso cometh unto me with a broken heart and a contrite spirit*, him will I baptize with fire and with the Holy Ghost, even as the Lamanites, because of their faith in me at the time of their conversion, were baptized with fire and the Holy Ghost, and they knew it not. (3 Nephi 9:19–20, emphasis added)

The sacrifice that is required of us is to offer to the Lord a broken heart and a contrite spirit. A broken heart is a softened, submissive, and willing heart. A contrite spirit is a humble, repentant spirit. Therefore, in essence, the foundational attribute—humility—is the sacrifice God asks of us.

Examples of Mere Mortals Who Were Humble

Some people, like my wife, seem to be naturally humble. Others, like me, need to work at it. At times I have thought that perhaps my struggle to be humble is tied to my competitive nature as a former athlete, but whatever the reason, I have always had a difficult time with this virtue. If you're naturally humble, you're fortunate. But, if you know how fortunate you are, perhaps you're not that humble. Still, I think you can tell if you have a problem with pride. When I was president of a military branch of the Church in Seoul, Korea, my first counselor was Dick Bergquist, a completely devoted, humble, self-effacing man. I learned much from serving with Brother Bergquist as I watched him serve faithfully, behind the scenes, without any fanfare. Elder Joseph B. Wirthlin, who passed away not long ago, strikes me as another man who was naturally humble. His desire was to do the Lord's will, and he did not seek the limelight.

Moses was a prince of Egypt. I don't know whether he was naturally humble or whether he had to work at it, but this much we know: "Now the man Moses was very meek, above all the men which were upon the face of the earth" (Numbers 12:3). Moses's humility is remarkable, given that he was one of the greatest leaders ever to live upon the earth.

Blessings of Humility

While it is often difficult to humble ourselves, there are many spiritual benefits of humility. Here is a list I have compiled of the blessings that come from humility (you may wish to look up each scripture and read it in its entirety):

- Be exalted (Matthew 23:12; Philippians 2:5–9).
- Be greatest in the kingdom of heaven (Matthew 18:4).
- Be lifted up (Psalm 147:6; James 4:10).
- Receive grace (1 Peter 5:5).
- Have the Lord extend His arm of mercy to you (Mosiah 29:20).
- Be prepared to meet God (Alma 5:27–28).
- Receive exceeding joy (Alma 27:18).
- Find rest to your soul (Alma 37:34).
- Be made strong, receive knowledge, and be blessed from on high (D&C 1:28).
- Be qualified to assist in the work (D&C 4:6; 12:8).
- Have peace in the Lord (D&C 19:23).
- Be qualified for baptism (D&C 20:37).
- Be forgiven of sins (D&C 61:2).
- Have the veil rent; see and know God (D&C 67:10).
- Receive a multiplicity of blessings (D&C 104:23).
- Have God soften the hearts of others in your life (D&C 104:80).
- Be victorious (D&C 104:82).
- Be led by God (D&C 112:10).
- Receive answers to prayers (D&C 112:10; see Joseph Smith—History).
- Have power to open the doors of the kingdom of God to the nations (D&C 112:21–22).
- Receive the Spirit, which shall manifest the truth (D&C 124:97).
- Learn wisdom and be enlightened (D&C 136:32–33).
- Have one's soul filled with joy and consolation (Helaman 3:35).
- Be visited with fire and the Holy Ghost and receive a remission of your sins (3 Nephi 12:2).

- Receive a great endowment and blessing (D&C 105:12).
- Have the Lord provide for your family (D&C 118:3).
- Not be destroyed (2 Chronicles 12:6–12).
- Be prepared to hear the word of God (Alma 32:6).
- Be blessed with rain on the face of the earth (Ether 9:35).
- Receive blessings of kingdom (D&C 61:37).
- Learn to know the Lord (See D&C 107:30–31).
- Inherit the earth (Psalm 37:11).
- Receive salvation (Psalm 149:4).
- Increase in joy in the Lord (Isaiah 29:19).
- Be fit to be numbered among the Lord's people (see Moroni 7:39).
- Have the Holy Ghost bear record of the truth (D&C 100:7–8).
- Receive the visitation of the Holy Ghost (Moroni 8:26).
- Exercise the power and influence of the Priesthood (see D&C 121:41–42).
- Be blessed (Alma 32:8).

I cannot imagine anyone who would not want these great and numerous blessings that come through being humble and meek.

Humility in the Modern World

Humility is not a trait that has been emphasized in our modern world. I have read many self-help books and have perused the covers of many more, but I have never seen a mass-market book about humility. That is why a discovery by business management guru Jim Collins was so surprising. Collins's landmark book entitled *Good to Great*, originally published in 2001, chronicles how eleven companies went from being good companies to being great companies. Here is what Collins and his team of researchers found:

> We were surprised, shocked really, to discover the type of leadership required for turning a good company into a great one. Compared to high-profile leaders with big personalities who make headlines and become celebrities, the good-to-great leaders seem to have come from Mars. Self-effacing, quiet, reserved, even shy—these leaders are a paradoxical blend of *personal humility* and professional will. They are more like Lincoln and Socrates than Patton or Caeser.[4]

The blessing and benefits of humility can even include success in a competitive business world, something many people never would have imagined.

How to Become and Remain Humble

How does a person become and remain humble? One way is by remembering. It is important to remember each day whom we are dependent on—the Lord—and to stay close to Him through consistent, worshipful, grateful prayer. There is a connection between gratitude and humility. Where there is true gratitude, there is humility. We must also constantly strive to be teachable and willing to receive chastisement, whether it comes from a leader, a parent, or from the Lord through His Spirit.

In a sense, humility may also be thought of as a lack of envy. As a high school student, I felt great jealousy at someone else's success. If another boy was selected as "most preferred man," I was upset. If another boy did better than me at sports, I resented the attention he received. It helped me in my pursuit of humility when I finally realized that someone else's victory was not my defeat; someone else's success was not my failure. Once I could rejoice in another's success without believing it somehow diminished me as a person, I felt I had found a key to humility.

Being a humble and meek person requires great self-control. In fact, President Harold B. Lee taught that meekness is a form of self-control:

> A meek man is defined as one who is not easily provoked or irritated and forbearing under injury or annoyance. Meekness is not synonymous with weakness. The meek man is the strong, the mighty, the man of complete self-mastery. He is the one who has the courage of his moral convictions, despite the pressure of the gang or the club. In controversy his judgment is the court of last-resort and his sobered counsel quells the rashness of the mob. He is humble-minded; he does not bluster. "He that is slow to anger is better than the mighty." (Proverbs 16:32.) He is a natural leader and is the chosen of army and navy, business and church to lead where other men follow. He is the 'salt' of the earth and shall inherit it.[5]

Yielding to the Holy Spirit will produce humility, as taught in one of the great verses of the Book of Mormon.

> For the natural man is an enemy to God, and has been from the fall of Adam, and will be, forever and ever, unless he yields to the enticings of the Holy Spirit, and putteth off the natural man and becometh a saint through the atonement of Christ the Lord, and becometh as a child, submissive, *meek, humble*, patient, full of love, willing to submit to all things which the Lord seeth fit to inflict upon him, even as a child doth submit to his father. (Mosiah 3:19, emphasis added)

Moroni taught that repentance and the remission of sins bring humility: "And the remission of sins bringeth meekness, and lowliness of heart; and because of meekness and lowliness of heart cometh the visitation of the Holy Ghost, which Comforter filleth with hope and perfect love, which love endureth by diligence unto prayer, until the end shall come, when all the saints shall dwell with God" (Moroni 8:26).

As we try to become humble, it also helps to recognize our weaknesses. The Lord promised: "And if men come unto me I will show unto them their weakness. I give unto men weakness that they may be humble; and my grace is sufficient for all men that humble themselves before me; for if they humble themselves before me, and have faith in me, then will I make weak things become strong unto them" (Ether 12:27).

My wife told me she is better able to retain her humility when she recognizes that anything she does well is a gift from God. It's true that when we use a talent that we have and that others lack, we can feel proud. However, all of us have talents and gifts, just not the same ones. When we do something well, we should not let that make us feel proud. Rather we should think of our talent as a gift of God, given to us to glorify His name and to bless the lives of His children. Considering our talents and gifts in this context can help us to use and develop them without being overly proud of them.

It seems to me that we get into trouble humility-wise when we compare ourselves to others. When we compare our strength to another's weakness, the natural result is that we become proud. For example, one brother may be a good public speaker and have no patience with fellow members who do not give fascinating talks in sacrament meeting. One sister may be organized and so become frustrated with people who can't seem to get their acts together. Yet the brother who is not a good public speaker may be a righteous and holy man. And the sister who is not organized may be a kind and nurturing mother.

The flip-side of comparing is also not helpful. When we compare our weakness to another's strength, the result is not pride, but rather discouragement. God does not want us to be proud, but He also doesn't want us to be discouraged. His message is one of hope and cheerfulness, not discouragement and depression.

To recap, we can become humble and retain our humility by doing the following:

- Striving to be grateful and teachable
- Avoiding and overcoming envy
- Exercising self-control
- Yielding to the enticings of the Holy Spirit
- Obtaining a remission of sins through repentance
- Recognizing our weaknesses
- Considering our talents and strengths as gifts from God
- Trying not to compare ourselves with others

If we become humble by doing the things mentioned above, then we'd better not be proud of our own humility, for as soon as we are, we'll have lost it!

The Nephite Pride Cycle

Most of us are familiar with the Nephite pride cycle that occurs again and again in the Book of Mormon. The Nephites are humble, so the Lord blesses them. Having received so many blessings, the Nephites become proud. Ultimately, when their pride leads to sin, they are destroyed or humbled through war and pestilence. And the cycle begins again.

Do we allow a similar pride cycle to exist in our lives? When things are hard, we often feel humble, turn to the Lord, and then become blessed for doing so. Having been greatly blessed, we soon become self-sufficient and forget the Lord. Then we get proud. We commit sins or make errors of judgment, and things become hard for us again. So we humble ourselves, and the cycle begins anew.

Let us learn from the Nephites and break the pride cycle. We can break it by being grateful, prayerful, repentant, and teachable; by having a lack of envy; and by having self-control. We can break it by yielding to the Holy Spirit.

Conclusion

As we conclude this discussion of humility, let us consider Alma's reminder of just how important it is for us to humble ourselves and become meek: "Could ye say, if ye were called to die at this time, within yourselves, that ye have been sufficiently humble? That your garments have been cleansed and made white through the blood of Christ, who will come to redeem his people from their sins? Behold, are ye stripped of pride? I say unto you, if ye are not ye are not prepared to meet God. Behold ye must prepare quickly; for the kingdom of heaven is soon at hand, and such an one hath not eternal life" (Alma 5:27–28).

If we are not stripped of pride, we are not prepared to meet God. If we are stripped of pride and are humble and meek, we are ready to move ahead in our quest for the divine virtues. And not only that, we will receive great blessings from our Heavenly Father, including peace, guidance, joy, and consolation. The Savior promised: "Learn of me, and listen to my words; *walk in the meekness of my Spirit*, and you shall have peace in me" (D&C 19:23, emphasis added). He has also commanded, "Be thou *humble*; and the Lord thy God shall *lead thee by the hand*, and give thee *answer to thy prayers*" (D&C 112:10, emphasis added).

And we learn, "Nevertheless they did fast and pray oft, and *did wax stronger and stronger in their humility*, and firmer and firmer in the faith of Christ, unto the *filling their souls with joy and consolation*, yea, even to the purifying and the sanctification of their hearts, which sanctification cometh because of their yielding their hearts unto God" (Helaman 3:35, emphasis added).

President Spencer W. Kimball, himself a model of humility, penned this poetic description of humility:

Humility is royalty without a crown,
Greatness in plain clothes,
Erudition without decoration,
Wealth without display,
Power without scepter or force,
Position demanding no preferential rights,

Greatness sitting in the congregation,
Prayer in closets and not in corners of the street,
Fasting in secret without publication,
Stalwartness without a label,
Supplication upon its knees,
Divinity riding an ass.[6]

Let us seek to be the humble person President Kimball described. If we are, we will be truly blessed and will be well on the way to Christian discipleship. We will have made a good start on our journey to becoming more like our Heavenly Father and His Son, Jesus Christ.

Summary

- Humility is the foundational attribute. If we are not humble, we will not even want to try to acquire the other divine virtues.
- Jesus Christ is the supreme example of humility and meekness. He sought His Father's will in all things. In effecting the Atonement, he suffered meekly on our behalf. Jesus was the perfect example of the servant-leader. Though He was the greatest of all, He was meek and lowly of heart.
- In Old Testament times, the people offered animal sacrifices. However, under the new covenant, we are asked to offer a broken heart and a contrite spirit (or, in other words, we are to be humble).
- There are many examples of mere mortals who are humble. Some seem to be naturally humble; others have to work at it.
- The scriptures outline numerous blessings of being humble, just a few of which are grace, mercy, joy, consolation, wisdom, forgiveness, guidance, and peace.
- Humility can even be a blessing in the modern business world. The most transformational business leaders tend to be humble and persistent, rather than proud and flamboyant.
- We can become humble and retain our humility if we (1) strive to be grateful and teachable; (2) avoid and overcome envy; (3) exercise self-control; (4) yield to the enticings of the Holy Spirit; (5) obtain a remission of sins through repentance); (6) recognize our weaknesses; (7) consider our strengths as gifts from God; and (8) avoid comparing ourselves to others.
- We must recognize the Nephite pride cycle as it exists in our life

and defeat it. By being continuously grateful and prayerful, we can avoid the self-sufficiency and willfulness that fuel the pride cycle.

- As we become humble, we will receive blessings and will be on the path to obtaining the other Christlike virtures.

Notes

1. Franklin, *The Autobiography of Benjamin Franklin*, 164; via Google books.
2. Bruce R. McConkie, *Doctrinal New Testament Commentary*, vol. 1 (Salt Lake City: Bookcraft, 1965), 500.
3. Alexander B. Morrison, *Zion: A Light in the Darkness* (Salt Lake City: Deseret Book, 1997), 65–66.
4. Jim Collins, *Good to Great* (New York City: HarperBusinesss, 2001), 12–13, emphasis added.
5. Harold B. Lee, *Decisions for Successful Living* (Salt Lake City: Deseret Book, 1973), 60.
6. Spencer W. Kimball, as quoted in Robert E. Wells, *The Mount and the Master* (Salt Lake City: Deseret Book, 1991), 33.

3

Obedience and Submissiveness

Thus we see that one of our primary labors in this life is to subordinate self, displace personal whims, and seek to have an eye single to the glory of God. True and lasting spiritual growth comes through seeking the mind of Christ, desiring to please the Father, and, like the Holy One, having our own will swallowed up in the will of heaven.

—*Robert L. Millet*[1]

When I was a missionary long ago, we studied Korean at the Language Training Mission at the Church College of Hawaii (now BYU—Hawaii). When I was there the LTM president was a wonderful man named Gene Hill. He has worked at the Missionary Training Center in Provo for most of his career. He is an inspirational teacher of the gospel. I once heard him use the following story regarding the *Mona Lisa*. I'm giving him credit for the story, because I heard it from him.

The *Mona Lisa* is the most famous painting in the world. It was painted in 1506 by the great artist and inventor Leonardo Da Vinci on a piece of pine wood. It now hangs in the Louvre in Paris. (I have personally had the privilege of viewing it on two occasions.)

You must queue up to view the painting. It is kept behind a protective glass, and it is lit only five minutes of every hour to prevent fading. No painting in art history has been so admired. This is due largely to the subject's enigmatic smile, which has caused much speculation.

According to President Hill's story, one day there were two men standing in the long line for the chance to briefly glimpse the world's greatest painting. One man was an art expert who had devoted much of his life to the study of painting. He had read widely on the subject and knew much about Da Vinci and his painting. The other man knew nothing about art whatsoever. After hours of waiting, the two men finally got their view of this great piece of art.

The expert was greatly moved by the *Mona Lisa*. Viewing it, for him, was a life-altering experience. But the novice was unimpressed and said, "I don't see what's so great about the *Mona Lisa*." The expert wisely responded, "But don't you wish you did?"

You see, the *Mona Lisa* is a great work of art. It is a masterpiece. The fact that an art novice cannot see why it would be is irrelevant. It is a masterpiece nevertheless.

As they go forth in the world, our missionaries meet people on a daily basis who do not think our gospel is important. They treat it as a thing of naught. They cannot see its value in their lives and have absolutely no interest in it. They don't see it as a masterpiece at all. However, the fact that a gospel novice does not recognize the value of the gospel does not render it worthless. Regardless of how it is received, the gospel is a pearl of great price.

Just as the art expert had to expend much effort over many years in order to understand and recognize the beauty of the *Mona Lisa*, so a person must study and live the gospel in order to recognize its beauty and value. We should never think less of the gospel because novices treat it lightly. We should become gospel experts through studying and living it. Obedience precedes a knowledge of the greatness of the gospel.

Obedience: Key to Blessings, Testimony, and Knowledge

President Spencer W. Kimball wisely observed that obedience also precedes the blessing:

> In faith we plant the seed, and soon we see the miracle of the blossoming. Men have often misunderstood and have reversed the process. They would have the harvest before the planting, the reward before the service, the miracle before the faith. Even the most demanding labor unions would hardly ask the wages before the labor. But many of us would have the vigor without the observance of the health laws, prosperity through the opened windows of heaven without the payment of our tithes. We would have close communion with our Father without fasting and praying; we would have rain in due season and peace in the land without observing the Sabbath and keeping the other commandments of the Lord. We would pluck the rose before planting the roots; we would harvest the grain before its planting and cultivating.[2]

Jesus taught this same principle: "My doctrine is not mine, but his that sent me. If any man will do his will, he shall know of the doctrine, whether it be of God, or whether I speak of myself" (John 7:16–17).

We have to live the doctrine before we can know whether it is of God. Obedience leads to knowledge that the doctrine is true. The Doctrine and Covenants teaches a similar concept: "There is a law, irrevocably decreed in heaven before the foundations of this world, upon which all blessings are predicated—And when we obtain any blessing from God, it is by obedience to that law upon which it is predicated" (D&C 130:20–21).

We may wish that we could receive the blessing first—and obey later. We may wish that we could harvest first—and plant later. We may wish that we could have the knowledge first—and study later. However, this simply is not the way it works. Faith precedes the miracle. Obedience precedes the blessing. Studying and living the gospel precede having a strong testimony of the gospel.

The gospel is a masterpiece, and we will know that it is if we study and obey it. But we cannot know it otherwise. Regardless of what gospel novices think or say, those of us who have tasted the goodness of the gospel, studied it, and strived to obey its teachings know that it is a far greater masterpiece than the *Mona Lisa*.

Obedience is the key to a testimony of the gospel. It is the prerequisite for receiving blessings. It is also how we obtain the Spirit in our lives. As the Apostle Peter taught, "Then Peter and the other apostles answered and said, We ought to obey God rather than men. The God of our fathers raised up Jesus, whom ye slew and hanged on a tree. Him hath God exalted with his right hand to be a Prince and a Saviour, for to give repentance to Israel, and forgiveness of sins. And we are his witnesses of these things; *and so is also the Holy Ghost, whom God hath given to them that obey him*" (Acts 5:29–32, emphasis added).

Obedience as a Way to Show Our Love to God

Obedience is also the best way—perhaps the only way— to express our love to God for His bounteous blessings, graciously given to us. There is a real connection between love and obedience.

Thanks to the expert questioning of a lawyer (and yes, I'm also a lawyer), we know what the two great commandments are. In the New Testament, we read of how Jesus taught them to the lawyer. "Then one of them, which was a lawyer, asked him a question, tempting him, and saying, Master, which is the great commandment in the law? Jesus said unto him, Thou shalt love the Lord thy God with all thy heart, and with all thy soul, and with all thy mind. This is the first and great commandment. And the second is like unto it, Thou shalt love thy neighbour as thyself. On these two commandments hang all the law and the prophets" (Matthew 22:35–40).

Here is my non-comprehensive list of why I love God:

- He gave me my life, and He sustains me daily with life and breath.
- He sent His Only Begotten Son to work out the Atonement for me. Because of this, I can be forgiven of my sins, I will be resurrected, and the Father and Son understand me and comfort me.
- He has given me the companionship of the Holy Ghost.
- He has been and will continue to be patient, long-suffering, and merciful with me.
- He gave me wonderful parents—a mother who taught me the gospel and a father who was a good example to me.
- He gave me a wonderful wife and children.
- He has given me the opportunity to grow by serving in the Church.
- He has given me associations with wonderful people—both inside and outside the Church—who have blessed my life.

- He allowed me to be born in a free country. I was able to gain an education, and this has blessed my life and the lives of my family members.
- He allowed me to be born in these last days when the gospel is on the earth and in a time of many opportunities.
- He has given me material blessings as well as spiritual blessings.

Think about why you love the Lord. What is on your list that I missed on mine? I am sure you have many reasons for loving God. How can we express that love? Several scriptures answer that question. For example, "If ye love me, keep my commandments" (John 14:15). "He that hath my commandments, and keepeth them, he it is that loveth me: and he that loveth me shall be loved of my Father, and I will love him, and will manifest myself to him" (John 14:21). And finally, "Ye are my friends, if ye do whatsoever I command you" (John 15:14).

We show our love to God by keeping His commandments. We become His friend by keeping His commandments. As Elder McConkie taught, our "love of God is measured in terms of obedience and service."[3]

When I served as a mission president, one of our missionaries, Elder Jared Peterson, was known for his exact obedience. I asked Elder Peterson why he was so strictly obedient, and he responded, "It's easy to say with my mouth that I love the Lord, but it is hard to show with my actions that I love Him. I have chosen to express my love to God by the way I act." These were wise words for such a young man. Actions truly do speak louder than words.

Commandments Are Not Grievous

Wait a minute! Aren't commandments restrictive and burdensome? You won't find any best-selling books about how to be more obedient. In our world, the focus is heavily tilted toward rights, not duties. But I want to proclaim that commandments are not restrictive and burdensome: "By this we know that we love the children of God, when we love God, and keep his commandments. For this is the love of God, that we keep his commandments: *and his commandments are not grievous*" (1 John 5:2–3, emphasis added).

Commandments can be thought of as protective boundaries given by a loving Heavenly Father. These boundaries are not given to fence us in and restrict us from having any fun, but rather to protect us from the pain and heartache that our omniscient Father knows lie outside those boundaries.

In fact, commandments are not to be avoided; they are to be sought after: "Yea, blessed are they whose feet stand upon the land of Zion, who have obeyed my gospel; for they shall receive for their reward the good things of the earth. . . . And they shall also be crowned with blessings from above, yea, *and with commandments not a few*, and with revelations in their time—they that are faithful and diligent before me" (D&C 59:3–4, emphasis added). If we obey, God will crown us "with commandments not a few." Why is this so? Because obedience to commandments will bring us even more blessings. Commandments are not grievous.

I will suggest merely a few examples of the blessings I have received from keeping the commandments:

Emotional Security through Keeping the Law of Chastity

It is a commandment to be faithful to one's spouse. Janet and I have been married for thirty-three years. During all that time, I have been faithful to her, and she has been faithful to me. Because of this, we have a very close relationship. We trust each other. We have the confidence of our children. Divorce has not plagued our family. We haven't suffered from sexually transmitted diseases. We have avoided the consequences of adultery that are described by Jacob in the Book of Mormon: "Ye have broken the hearts of your tender wives, and lost the confidence of your children, because of your bad examples before them; and the sobbings of their hearts ascend up to God against you. And because of the strictness of the word of God, which cometh down against you, many hearts died, pierced with deep wounds" (Jacob 2:35).

Financial Security through Paying a Full Tithe

By paying tithing, we open the windows of heaven. Janet and I have always paid our tithing, and the Lord has always blessed us when we needed it—sometimes in miraculous ways.

Once when we were in law school, we were out of money, except for our tithing, with a week to go before our next paycheck. We paid our tithing and hoped for a miracle. Within hours, and totally out of the blue, my less-active aunt visited our student apartment with sack-loads of food, saying she had felt impressed to do so. She never gave us food before or after that day. We knew without a doubt that she had been an instrument in God's hands to bless us for our faithfulness in paying our tithing.

Health

Keeping the Word of Wisdom promotes physical and spiritual health. I have experienced both by observing this commandment. Not only are our physical bodies healthier, but our bodies are more fit to be receptacles for the Spirit of God when we observe the Word of Wisdom.

Happiness

I believe my life has been happy as a result of obeying the commandments of God. Joseph Smith taught that "happiness is the object and design of our existence; and will be the end thereof, if we pursue the path that leads to it; and this path is virtue, uprightness, faithfulness, holiness, and keeping all the commandments of God. But we cannot keep all the commandments without first knowing them, and we cannot expect to know all, or more than we now know unless we comply with or keep those we have already received."[4]

Missionary Blessings

Those of us who have served full-time missions know from experience that missionaries are blessed when they obey the mission rules. Henry B. Eyring taught this concept as follows, "The great opportunity in teaching obedience to missionaries is to help them see the connection between the Savior, the companionship of the Spirit, and love. It is to teach them that obedience to the commands of the Father and His Son out of love for Them brings the Spirit. The companionship of the Spirit will bring light and truth, the foundation of successful missionary work and of a happy life."[5]

Gifts of the Spirit

Another magnificent blessing of obedience is that it entitles us to receive the gifts of the Spirit, which are outlined in 1 Corinthians 12, Doctrine and Covenants 46, and Moroni 10. The Lord said that these gifts are "given for the benefit of those who love me and keep all my commandments, and him that seeketh so to do" (D&C 46:9). What a blessing to know that the gifts of the Spirit are given not only for the benefit of those who keep the commandments, but also for the benefit of those of us who seek to do so but fall short on so many occasions.

Example of Jesus

We have talked extensively of the blessings of obedience. Now let us turn to the example of Jesus, for, after all, His is the finest example of obedience and submissiveness.

Jesus was the only person who ever lived on the earth that did not need to have His sins remitted. He did not need to be washed clean. And yet, he was baptized. "Then cometh Jesus from Galilee to Jordan unto John, to be baptized of him. But John forbad him, saying, I have need to be baptized of thee, and comest thou to me? And Jesus answering said unto him, Suffer it to be so now: for thus it becometh us to fulfil all righteousness. Then he suffered him" (Matthew 3:13–15).

In the Book of Mormon, Nephi clarifies the reason for the Lord's desire to be baptized: "And now, I would ask of you, my beloved brethren, wherein the Lamb of God did fulfill all righteousness in being baptized by water? Know ye not that he was holy? But notwithstanding he being holy, he showeth unto the children of men that, according to the flesh he humbleth himself before the Father, and witnesseth unto the Father that he would be obedient unto him in keeping his commandments" (2 Nephi 31:6–7).

The Lord was baptized in order to show the Father His desire to be obedient. In fact, His whole desire was to do the will of his Father, as portrayed in the following scriptures. "Jesus saith unto them, My meat is to do the will of him that sent me, and to finish his work" (John 4:34). He also said, "I can of mine own self do nothing: as I hear, I judge: and my judgment is just; because I seek not mine own will, but the will of the Father which hath sent me" (John 5:30). "For," said He, "I came down from heaven, not to do mine own will, but the will of him that sent me" (John 6:38).

The most magnificent example of obedience in all of history is the Lord's Atonement. With the suffering of Gethsemane and the cross looming before Him, "he went a little further, and fell on his face, and prayed, saying, O my Father, if it be possible, let this cup pass from me: nevertheless not as I will, but as thou wilt" (Matthew 26:39). The cup could not pass, and Jesus fulfilled the will of His Father.

The Atonement is the ultimate act of submissiveness, as explained in two Book of Mormon scriptures. "Yea, even so he shall be led, crucified, and slain, the flesh becoming subject even unto death, the will of the Son being swallowed up in the will of the Father" (Mosiah 15:7). "And behold, I am the light and the life of the world; and I have drunk out of that bitter cup which the Father hath given me, and have glorified the Father in taking upon me the sins of the world, in the which I have suffered the will of the Father in all things from the beginning" (3 Nephi 11:11).

Examples of Mere Mortals

The scriptures are replete with examples of mortals who have demonstrated their obedience and have been greatly blessed. For example, Abraham was willing to offer his only son in obedience to God's command, but fortunately there was a ram in the thicket (see Genesis 22:10–13). Blessed for his obedience, Abraham became the father of nations. Similarly, Nephi was steadfast in going and doing what the Lord commanded (1 Nephi 3:7). He became the leader of a great people.

Alma the Younger is also a great example to us. He had been a wicked and idolatrous man. However, he was later praised by the same angel who had first rebuked him. "Blessed art thou, Alma; therefore, lift up thy head and rejoice, for thou hast great cause to rejoice; for thou hast been faithful in keeping the commandments of God from the time which thou receivedst thy first message from him. Behold, I am he that delivered it unto you" (Alma 8:15). After having been rejected and spat upon by the people of Ammonihah, "he returned speedily to the land of Ammonihah" to try again at the direction of the angel (Alma 8:18).

Another great example of obedience is Nephi, the son of Helaman. This Nephi was tireless in his service to God and consistently obedient. As a result, he was given the sealing power because the Lord knew he could always be trusted to act correctly.

> And it came to pass as he was thus pondering in his heart, behold, a voice came unto him saying: Blessed art thou, Nephi, for those things which thou hast done; for I have beheld how thou hast

> with unwearyingness declared the word, which I have given unto thee, unto this people. And thou hast not feared them, and hast not sought thine own life, *but hast sought my will, and to keep my commandments*. And now, because thou hast done this with such unwearyingness, behold, I will bless thee forever; and I will make thee mighty in word and in deed, in faith and in works; yea, even that all things shall be done unto thee according to thy word, for thou shalt not ask that which is contrary to my will. (Helaman 10:3–5, emphasis added)

Becoming Obedient

How do we become obedient? As noted in Chapter 2, obedience presupposes humility. Arrogant people are less inclined to bend their will to the will of the Lord. So the first thing we need to do is to seek after humility.

Next, we need to test the fruits of obedience by obeying. Jesus said: "My doctrine is not mine, but his that sent me. If any man will do his will, he shall know of the doctrine, whether it be of God, or whether I speak of myself" (John 7:16–17). If we do the will of the Father by keeping one of His commandments, we will know that it is true, and we will receive the blessings associated with that commandment. When we do this enough times, we become absolutely convinced that God has given us commandments to bless us.

I have learned over many years of trying to keep the commandments that, ironically, submitting my will to the will of God does not bring me grief or anguish; it does not weigh me down; it does not inhibit my freedom. Rather, it makes my heart light and brings me deep and abiding happiness and peace. The commandments truly are not grievous. Learning this lesson, through experience, increases our desire to be obedient and submissive to our Heavenly Father.

Conclusion

One of the objectives of our earth life is to live so that we can go to the celestial world where the righteous dwell. There we will find the patriarchs Abraham, Isaac, and Jacob; the Prophet Joseph Smith, Heber C. Kimball and Brigham Young; the Apostles Peter, James, John, and Paul; the Book of Mormon prophets, including Alma and both Nephis;

and the numerous righteous and faithful brothers and sisters who have lived throughout the history of the earth. How comfortable will we be in their presence if we were not enthusiastically obedient, faithful, and submissive here on earth? In my opinion, if we're not going to be comfortable in their presence, we won't *be* in their presence.

We know that God's "work and glory" is "to bring to pass the immortality and eternal life of man" (Moses 1:39). This is God's mission statement. There is a parallel scripture in the Doctrine and Covenants that tells us what our work is as his children: "Behold, this is your work, to keep my commandments, yea, with all your might, mind and strength" (D&C 11:20). That is our mission statement.

Let us fulfill our mission statement, then, by keeping the commandments with all our might, mind, and strength. In so doing, we will become more like Christ, who allowed His will to be swallowed up in the will of His Father, and we will receive the numerous blessings that flow directly from obedience.

President Boyd K. Packer has taught in several settings that the ultimate expression of obedience and submission is to yield back to Heavenly Father His gift of agency—giving Him something He would never take forcefully from us.[6] As we yield our will—our agency—to God, saying, in essence, that our only desire is to do His will, we become true servants of the Father and more like our Lord Jesus Christ, who allowed His will to be swallowed up in the will of His Father.

Summary

- To know the truthfulness of the gospel, we have to study and live it.
- Obedience precedes the blessing.
- Obedience is the best way to show our love for God.
- Commandments are not grievous and burdensome. In fact, they are to be sought after because keeping commandments brings blessings.
- Commandments are boundaries given to us by an omniscient Father to protect us from the pain and heartache He knows lie outside those boundaries.
- Obedience brings the Spirit and many other blessings.
- Jesus set the best example of obedience and submissiveness. He

came to the earth to do the will of His Father. He was baptized to show His obedience. He kept all the commandments. He submitted His will to that of His Father by suffering for our sins in Gethsemane and on the cross.

- The prophets in the Bible and Book of Mormon are examples of mortals who were obedient to the Lord's commandments and who were greatly blessed.
- Humility is a prerequisite to obedience. As we keep the commandments, we will know that they are from God and that they are good. Our testimonies will continue to grow.
- Unless we are obedient, we will likely not be comfortable in a celestial world filled with individuals who have valiantly and faithfully kept the commandments and served the Lord.
- God's work is to bring to pass the immorality and eternal life of man. Our work is to keep His commandments with all our might, mind, and strength.
- The ultimate expression of obedience and submission is to voluntarily yield back to Heavenly Father something He would never forcefully take from us—His gift of agency—thereby saying, in essence, that our only desire is to do His will.

Notes

1. Robert L. Millet, *Alive in Christ: The Miracle of Spiritual Rebirth* (Salt Lake City: Deseret Book, 1997), 184.
2. Spencer W. Kimball in Conference Report, October 1952, 47.
3. Bruce R. McConkie, *Mormon Doctrine*, second edition (Salt Lake City: Bookcraft, 1966), 540.
4. Joseph Smith, *Teachings of the Prophet Joseph Smith*, 255.
5. Henry B. Eyring, "A Life Founded in Light and Truth," *Ensign*, July 2001, 12–13.
6. Boyd K. Packer, *That All May Be Edified* (Salt Lake City: Bookcraft, 1982), 257.

4

Faith and Hope

We must be careful, as we seek to become more and more godlike, that we do not become discouraged and lose hope. Becoming Christlike is a lifetime pursuit and very often involves growth and change that is slow, almost imperceptible. The scriptures record remarkable accounts of men whose lives changed dramatically, in an instant, as it were: Alma the Younger, Paul on the road to Damascus, Enos praying far into the night, King Lamoni. . . .

But we must be cautious as we discuss these remarkable examples. Though they are real and powerful, they are the exception more than the rule. For every Paul, for every Enos, and for every King Lamoni, there are hundreds and thousands of people who find the process of repentance much more subtle, much more imperceptible. Day by day they move closer to the Lord, little realizing they are building a godlike life. They live quiet lives of goodness, service, and commitment. They are like the Lamanites, who the Lord said "were baptized with fire and with the Holy Ghost, and they knew it not." (3 Nephi 9:20)

We must not lose hope. Hope is an anchor to the souls of men. . . . The Lord is pleased with every effort, even the tiny, daily ones in which we strive to be more like Him. Though we may see that we have far to go on the road to perfection, we must not give up hope.

—*Ezra Taft Benson*[1]

I mentioned earlier that as a young man headed to South Korea on a mission, I did my language study at the Language Training Mission (or LTM), located on the campus of what is now BYU—Hawaii. I don't mind telling you it was hard to concentrate on a difficult Asian language while living in paradise. We studied and memorized all day—and then had a period called "retention" in the evening when we tried to "retain" what we had poured into our heads during that day. Between study and retention were dinner at 5:00 pm and devotional at 6:00 pm. Retention started promptly at 7:00 pm.

Devotional was held in a large room that seated the 110 missionaries going to Asia, the large majority of whom were going to Japan, with a few each going to Korea, Taiwan, and Thailand. Most of the seating in the room consisted of hard folding chairs, but interestingly, there was a sofa at the very back of the room. If you hurried from dinner at the cafeteria, you had a chance of sitting on the soft sofa.

One evening my companion, Elder Kim Nilsen, and I arrived early enough for the coveted seat. The speaker, to my chagrin, was a Ben Stein–like teacher from the institute and was known for his long, monotone lectures. He began: "Today I will speak about faith. Faith is very important. . . ."

I had to do something to spice up the time, and I noticed that there was a clock on the back wall and that its cord ran down to a socket near the sofa. I suggested that Elder Nilsen unplug the cord. He was afraid of getting in trouble, but I talked him into it. I told him not to leave it unplugged, or everyone would notice, but rather to pull it out for a minute and then plug it in for a minute. Well, Elder Nilsen performed flawlessly, and in the course of one hour, he slowed the clock down by 30 minutes.

The speaker paid no attention to the clock, for he had given the same lecture to every LTM group for years. The elders in the folding chairs did notice, though, and as they looked at the clock and compared their watches, one by one they changed their watches to match the clock. It took great self-discipline on my part not to laugh when they did this.

As the teacher was concluding, he noticed the clock and said, "Wow, I've given this lecture a lot, and it's always taken the full time. Well, let me summarize the important things I've said." He couldn't fill all the time, so a counselor in the mission presidency had the group sing hymns until the clock said 7:00 (which was really 7:30).

Needless to say, we had an extra short retention period that evening, yet somehow I still managed to learn Korean.

As I mentioned, the institute teacher started his lecture by saying, "Faith is important." At the time I thought this sounded like an incredibly boring topic, taught by an incredibly boring teacher. However, he was right about faith. And in retrospect, I wish I'd listened to his lecture instead of playing a practical joke. Faith is so important that it is one of the divine virtues.

Faith Defined

The Apostle Paul taught, "Now faith is the substance of things hoped for, the evidence of things not seen" (Hebrews 11:1). Alma taught, "And now as I said concerning faith—faith is not to have a perfect knowledge of things; therefore if ye have faith ye hope for things which are not seen, which are true" (Alma 32:21). And Moroni added, "And now, I, Moroni, would speak somewhat concerning these things; I would show unto the world that faith is things which are hoped for and not seen; wherefore, dispute not because ye see not, for ye receive no witness until after the trial of your faith" (Ether 12:6). As we learn from these scriptures, hope is a part of faith and, as we will discuss later, faith is also a part of hope. Moroni helped make this clear when he said, "How is it that ye can attain unto faith, save ye shall have hope?" (Moroni 7:40).

Faith is not a perfect knowledge of things, but faith leads to knowledge when we plant the seed of faith and try the experiment, as taught by Alma (see Alma 32:26–35).

Faith in the Lord Jesus Christ is the first principle of the gospel. Jesus is the "author and finisher of our faith" (Hebrews 12:2; Moroni 6:4). Faith is a principle of action; it leads to repentance, baptism, and the Gift of the Holy Ghost. It takes faith to endure to the end. Faith is the pathway to salvation and eternal life.

The *Encyclopedia of Mormonism* states: "True faith is belief plus action. Faith implies not only the mental assent or cognition of belief but also its implementation. Beliefs in things both spiritual and secular impel people to act. Failure to act on the teachings and commandments of Christ implies absence of faith in him. Faith in Jesus Christ impels people to act in behalf of Christ, to follow his example, to do his works."[2]

The Apostle James, brother of our Lord, taught: "Even so faith, if it hath not works, is dead, being alone. Yea, a man may say, Thou hast faith, and I have works: shew me thy faith without thy works, and I will shew thee my faith by my works" (James 2:17–18).

Faith is a principle of power. President Boyd K. Packer has taught that "fear is the opposite of faith."[3] After the Lord had rebuked the wind and the sea, He asked his disciples, "Why are ye so fearful? How is it that ye have no faith?" (Mark 4:40). I believe that in this regard faith is like love, for as John taught: "There is no fear in love; but perfect love casteth out fear" (1 John 4:18). Faith can cast out fear.

Faith Demonstrated

Speaking of the power of faith, the scriptures show many examples of faith in action, which I will now share in non-chronological order. In addition to those listed, we know that all miracles are wrought by faith, or in other words, faith precedes the miracle (see Ether 12:16). By faith, the following miracles occurred:

- Christ showed Himself to the fathers after He had risen from the dead (Ether 12:7).
- Alma and Amulek caused the prison to tumble to the earth (Ether 12:12).
- Ammon and his brethren wrought a great miracle among the Lamanites (Ether 12:15).
- The Brother of Jared saw the finger of the Lord (Ether 12:20–21).
- The world was framed by the word of God (Hebrews 11:3).
- Enoch was translated (Hebrews 11:5).
- The three disciples received the promise they would not suffer death (Ether 12:17).
- Abel offered a more excellent sacrifice than Cain (Hebrews 11:4).
- The walls of Jericho fell down (Hebrews 11:30).
- Noah prepared an ark (and it wasn't even raining at the time) (Hebrews 11:7).
- Sarah conceived when she was past the age for child-bearing (Hebrews 11:11).
- Abraham was willing to offer up Isaac as a sacrifice (Hebrews

11:17). (Fortunately for him, Abraham was not required to go through with his sacrifice, but there was no ram in the thicket when our Heavenly Father had to sacrifice His Beloved Son.)

- Moses left his luxurious life to suffer affliction with the people of God, leading them through the Red Sea as though it was dry land (Hebrews 11:23–29).

Paul's letter to the Hebrews also teaches us that it is by faith that we are able to please God, for it is impossible to please Him without faith (see Hebrews 11:6).

In our time, faith prompted Joseph Smith to ask which church he should join—and by faith he was an instrument in the Lord's hand to bring about the great Restoration of the gospel. There is no doubt that faith played an important role in the prayer he gave that ultimately launched a dispensation. Before praying, young Joseph read and pondered this New Testament scripture: "If any of you lack wisdom, let him ask of God, that giveth to all men liberally, and upbraideth not; and it shall be given him. But let *him ask in faith, nothing wavering*. For he that wavereth is like a wave of the sea driven with the wind and tossed" (James 1:5–6, emphasis added).

In my own life, it was by faith that as a frightened young father, I blessed my sick baby daughter, Laura, in the middle of the night and she was healed immediately. I am sure that the faith-filled prayers of her worried mother were also efficacious in her behalf.

By faith I blessed (and released from mortality) my aged grandmother the night before she was to have her legs amputated. She was then relieved of suffering and allowed to slip peacefully out of this life. This was a great relief to my mother, who could not bear to think of her aged mother, with no prospect of long-term recovery, having her legs amputated.

What has happened in your life as a result of faith in the Lord Jesus Christ? And what will happen in your future?

As you think of the examples of faith cited above, consider this verse from the Book of Mormon: "And neither at any time hath any wrought miracles until after their faith; wherefore they first believed in the Son of God" (Ether 12:18). To borrow an oft-quoted line (and book title) from President Kimball, "Faith precedes the miracle."[4]

Faith Leads to Strength

Being a principle of power, faith can help turn weaknesses to strengths. In Chapter 2, I said that humility is the foundational attribute. There is an interesting result when humility is combined with faith. In one of the great chapters of the Book of Mormon, we read: "And if men come unto me I will show unto them their weakness. I give unto men weakness that they may be humble; and my grace is sufficient for all men that humble themselves before me; for if they humble themselves before me, and have faith in me, then will I make weak things become strong unto them" (Ether 12:27).

From this scripture, we can derive a powerful formula for positive change:

Humility + Faith = Strength

Let me share a dramatic example of this formula at work in the life of Enoch. What a privilege it is to learn more of Enoch from the Pearl of Great Price. God called Enoch to His work, commanding him to prophesy unto the people and command them to repent (see Moses 6:27–30). This was Enoch's initial response: "And when Enoch had heard these words, he bowed himself to the earth, before the Lord, and spake before the Lord, saying: Why is it that I have found favor in thy sight, and am but a lad, and all the people hate me; *for I am slow of speech*; wherefore am I thy servant?" (Moses 6:31, emphasis added).

But Enoch went forth and did what the Lord commanded—and he had faith. You can also see from his response that he was humble. This was the result of his humility + faith:

> And so great was the *faith* of Enoch that he led the people of God, and their enemies came to battle against them; and *he spake the word of the Lord, and the earth trembled, and the mountains fled*, even according to his command; and the rivers of water were turned out of their course; and the roar of the lions was heard out of the wilderness; and all nations feared greatly, *so powerful was the word of Enoch, and so great was the power of the language which God had given him*. (Moses 7:13, emphasis added)

He may have been slow of speech when he received his calling, but Enoch's humility and faith led him to great priesthood power and great power of speech. Enoch's weakness (at least what he had perceived as a weakness) had become his strength. In Chapter 7, on temperance, I will relate a less dramatic story from my own life of how the humility + faith formula turned one of my weaknesses into a strength.

FAITH LEADS TO POWER

Our faith in the Lord Jesus Christ unlocks the enabling power known as His grace. Continuing in Ether 12, we read: "And now, I would commend you to seek this Jesus of whom the prophets and apostles have written, that the grace of God the Father, and also the Lord Jesus Christ, and the Holy Ghost, which beareth record of them, may be and abide in you forever. Amen" (Ether 12:41).

Seeking Jesus in faith brings into play the grace of God (see Romans 5:2). The best explanation of grace comes from the Bible Dictionary, which defines grace as follows:

> Grace. A word that occurs frequently in the New Testament, especially in the writings of Paul. The main idea of the word is *divine means of help or strength*, given through the bounteous mercy and love of Jesus Christ.
>
> It is through the grace of the Lord Jesus, made possible by his atoning sacrifice, that mankind will be raised in immortality. . . . It is likewise through the grace of the Lord that individuals, through faith in the atonement of Jesus Christ and repentance of their sins, *receive strength and assistance to do good works that they otherwise would not be able to maintain if left to their own means.* This grace is an enabling power that allows men and women to lay hold on eternal life and exaltation after they have expended their own best efforts. . . .
>
> Grace, then, is a divine means of help or strength. It is an enabling power. Total effort on our part is still required, but with our full effort and with the grace of God, we can do works that we would otherwise not be able to do if left to our own means. (emphasis added)

Moroni described the relationship between faith and power in this way: "And Christ hath said: If ye will have faith in me ye shall have power to do whatsoever thing is expedient in me" (Moroni 7:33). And the Apostle Paul said: "I can do all things through Christ which strengtheneth me" (Philippians 4:13).

HOPE

Now let's turn our attention to hope. In our time, we have heard civil rights leaders urge their followers to "keep hope alive." That's a good idea for all of us. We truly should always keep hope alive.

When I served as a mission president, I once asked our zone leaders to share their opinions of what some of our weaknesses in the mission were. Several of them answered, "Our missionaries are obedient and diligent, but they are without hope." I asked what they meant. They continued: "Before we received our mission calls, we thought, 'If I go to an English-speaking mission, I'll become a scripture scholar on my mission. If I go to Latin America, I will baptize, baptize, baptize. But if I go to Asia, I will become humble—for I will have to learn a hard language and I won't have much success.' " Their mindset was without hope—"I'll work hard and do my best, but it won't do any good, because no one in Asia is interested in the gospel."

To make a long story short, over the ensuing months, we brought hope to life and kept it alive, and several important things happened. First, the number of contacts went way up. Second, the number of discussions also went way up. And finally, the number of baptisms went . . . slightly up. We could not override agency, but in the spirit of hope, we had the opportunity to share the gospel with more people. We were happier and blessed for it. And I repeat: the number of baptisms went *up*, at least slightly, and those additional converts were greatly blessed because of our hope.

I cannot adequately express what a difference it makes in a missionary's life when the number of discussions he or she is teaching goes from one a week to one a day or even two or three a day. Even though the baptism harvest was only slightly greater, the experience of being able to teach regularly was a blessing in the life of every missionary in our mission. Our missionaries were already diligent. The change came about because of attitude and, even more important, because of our faith- and hope-filled prayers to God for opportunities to share His gospel. Our experience helped us internalize the teaching of this scripture: "And no one can assist in this work except he shall be humble and full of love, having faith, hope, and charity, being temperate in all things, whatsoever shall be entrusted to his care" (D&C 12:8).

Our ability to assist in the work improved when we did it with hope, for "faith, hope, charity and love, with an eye single to the glory of God, qualify [a missionary] for the work" (D&C 4:5). More people had the opportunity to hear the gospel when we performed our missionary labors with hope.

I said earlier that hope is a part of faith and faith is a part of hope. It's true—hope does come from faith. Take a look at these two scriptures: "Wherefore, *whoso believeth in God might with surety hope for a better world*, yea, even a place at the right hand of God, *which hope cometh of faith*, maketh an anchor to the souls of men, which would make them sure and steadfast, always abounding in good works, being led to glorify God" (Ether 12:4, emphasis added). And, "Wherefore, if a man have faith he must needs have hope; *for without faith there cannot be any hope*" (Moroni 7:42, emphasis added).

Faith causes us to hope for a better world—to hope for salvation and eternal life through the Atonement of Jesus Christ: "And what is it that ye shall hope for? Behold I say unto you that ye shall have hope through the atonement of Christ and the power of his resurrection, to be raised unto life eternal, and this because of your faith in him according to the promise" (Moroni 7:41).

Peter put it this way: "Blessed be the God and Father of our Lord Jesus Christ, which according to his abundant mercy hath begotten us again unto a *lively hope* by the resurrection of Jesus Christ from the dead" (1 Peter 1:3, emphasis added).

And Moroni used these beautiful words to describe it: "And I also remember that thou hast said that thou hast prepared a house for man, yea, even among the mansions of thy Father, in which man might have *a more excellent hope*; wherefore man must hope, or he cannot receive an inheritance in the place which thou hast prepared" (Ether 12:32, emphasis added).

My father died in 1998, my mother in 1999. I miss them terribly, even today, but I learned through their passing that love is stronger than death. It is my faith in the Lord Jesus Christ, developed and nurtured over many years, that gives me the "perfect brightness of hope" (2 Nephi 31:20) that I will see them again. This "lively hope," this "excellent hope," gives me peace and comfort. Jesus is the Hope of Israel (see Jeremiah 14:8; Joel 3:16). God is the God of hope (Romans 15:13). Heavenly Father and His Son, Jesus Christ, are my source of hope—both for myself and for my beloved family members. It is because of this hope that I look forward to the future and do not despair (see Moroni 10:22).

In the scriptures, hope usually relates to the happiness that will come from the resurrection, salvation, and an eternal life in the mansions of our Father (see Alma 13:29). However, as I noted earlier, hope helped us do a better job in our callings as missionaries. And hope is the optimism that we naturally develop when we have faith in the Lord Jesus Christ. President Hinckley was such a hopeful person. He often encouraged us to "accentuate the positive." President Henry B. Eyring said of President Hinckley: "His optimism stemmed from his unwavering faith in Jesus Christ and the power of His Atonement."[5]

Developing Faith and Hope

As we have learned, faith and hope are inseparably connected. Hope leads to faith, which leads to even greater hope. What can we do to develop greater faith and hope, these two divine, interconnected attributes of Christ?

In Romans 10:17, we learn that "faith cometh by hearing, and hearing by the word of God." We hear the word of God by studying the scriptures regularly and by listening to the teachings of the living prophets, leaders, and our fellow members of the Church. The word of God feeds our faith and makes it grow stronger and brighter. The scriptures can also help us develop hope: "For whatsoever things were written aforetime were written for our learning, that we through patience and comfort of the scriptures might have hope" (Romans 15:4).

In one sense, faith is a gift. It is referred to in the scriptures as a gift of the spirit (see Moroni 10:10; D&C 46:13, 19–20; 1 Corinthians 12:9). We are told that we can seek for the best gifts (see D&C 46:8). Therefore, it is appropriate and desirable to ask Heavenly Father for the gift of faith.

Since faith is belief plus action, we should follow Alma's inspired teachings about planting the seed of faith (see Alma 32:26–43). Alma invites us to experiment on his words by exercising a particle of faith, just desiring to believe and giving belief a place in our heart. He tells us to plant the seed of faith in our hearts and not cast it out by unbelief or by resisting the Spirit of the Lord. If we do this, faith will begin to swell within our breasts. When we feel this, we will know that this is a good seed, for it will begin to enlarge our souls, enlighten our understandings, and be delicious to us. Our faith will increase, and we will know it. This seed is real; it is light; and whatsoever is light is good. We need to continue to nourish the seed of faith, which will ultimately grow into a tree of everlasting life. But we must never neglect the tree, or it will die—not because it wasn't good, but because we ceased nourishing it with diligence and patience.

Nourishing the seed (and subsequently the tree) of faith involves regular scripture study, daily heartfelt prayer, obedience to the commandments, repentance of sins, and service to others. This type of nourishment makes the tree grow stronger and stronger until it yields its fruit of eternal life.

Now let's look at developing hope. In Chapter 2, I wrote of humility as the foundational attribute. Humility leads to hope, as we learn from the Book of Mormon: "And the remission of sins bringeth meekness, and lowliness of heart; and because of meekness and lowliness of heart cometh the visitation of the Holy Ghost, which Comforter filleth with hope and perfect love, which love endureth by diligence unto prayer, until the end shall come, when all the saints shall dwell with God" (Moroni 8:26).

Repentance leads to humility, which leads to the visitation of the Holy Ghost. The Comforter then fills us with hope and perfect love. Ultimately, the result is being able to dwell with God. The connection between humility and hope (and faith too!) is confirmed when we read: "And again, behold I say unto you that he cannot have faith and hope, save he shall be meek, and lowly of heart" (Moroni 7:43).

Elder Bruce R. McConkie taught that "hope is born of righteousness."[6] Thus, by continuously repenting of our sins and striving to be obedient to the gospel, we increase in hope.

Experiences and trials can lead to hope, as Paul taught in the book of Romans: "And not only so, but we glory in tribulations also: knowing that tribulation worketh patience; And patience, experience; and experience, hope" (Romans 5:3–4). Paul must have known this personally because after his conversion he had many trials. No one has more tribulation and trials than the prophets of God, yet interestingly, no one has more brightness of hope than the prophets of God. In my life, I have known a number of less conspicuous Saints who have borne well trials of the most difficult kind—and they too have come to possess a lively hope for a better world through the Atonement of Christ.

Conclusion

Faith and hope are interconnected divine virtues. Hope is part of the definition of faith. And faith leads to greater hope. Without faith, hope, and charity (which will be discussed in the next chapter), we can do nothing (see D&C 18:19). With faith, hope, and charity, we will always abound in good works (see Alma 7:24). Faith, hope, and charity lead us to the fountain of all righteousness (see Ether 12:28). Without faith, we cannot please God (see D&C 63:11).

We will have hope and be partakers of the gift of eternal life if we will but have faith (see Ether 12:9). For as Nephi taught: "Wherefore, ye must press forward with a steadfastness in Christ, *having a perfect brightness of hope*, and a love of God and of all men. Wherefore, if ye shall press forward, feasting upon the word of Christ, and endure to the end, behold, thus saith the Father: Ye shall have eternal life" (2 Nephi 31:20, emphasis added).

Summary

- Faith is a hope for things which are not seen, but which are true.
- Hope is part of faith and faith is part of hope.
- Faith is not perfect knowledge, but faith leads to knowledge.
- Faith in the Lord Jesus Christ is the first principle of the gospel; it leads to repentance, baptism, the Gift of the Holy Ghost, and enduring to the end.
- Faith is belief plus action. Thus, faith without works is dead.
- Faith is a principle of power. Faith drives out fear.
- By faith, many mighty miracles have been wrought. Faith precedes the miracle.
- Faith can turn weaknesses to strengths. The scriptural formula for this is Humility + Faith = Strength.
- Faith in Christ unlocks grace, the enabling power. If we have faith, we have the power to do whatever is expedient.
- No one can assist (at least not effectively) in the work (especially missionary work) unless he or she has hope. Hope is one of the qualifications for missionary work.
- Faith in Christ causes us to hope for a better world. We have confidence that we can obtain eternal life. In my case, it gives me hope that I will see my deceased parents again.

- Hope, as taught in the scriptures, usually relates to the prospect of eternal life. However, hope is the natural optimism a person has when he or she has faith in Christ.
- We develop faith by hearing the word of God, by asking for the gift of faith, and by experimenting with faith as taught by Alma.
- Repentance and humility lead to the Spirit, and the Comforter is a source of hope. Hope is born of righteousness and also from experience and trials.

Notes

1. Ezra Taft Benson, "A Mighty Change of Heart," *Ensign*, Oct. 1989, 2–5.
2. *Encyclopedia of Mormonism*, ed. Daniel H. Ludlow (New York: Macmillan, 1992), 483–84.
3. Boyd K. Packer, "Do Not Fear," *Ensign*, May 2004, 77.
4. Spencer W. Kimball, *Faith Precedes the Miracle* (Salt Lake City: Deseret Book, 1972).
5. Henry B. Eyring, "Things Will Work Out," *Liahona*, Apr. 2008, 26–28.
6. Bruce R. McConkie, *Mormon Doctrine*, 365.

5

Charity and Love

Beloved, let us love one another: for love is of God; and every one that loveth is born of God, and knoweth God. He that loveth not knoweth not God; for God is love. In this was manifested the love of God toward us, because that God sent his only begotten Son into the world, that we might live through him. Herein is love, not that we loved God, but that he loved us, and sent his Son to be the propitiation for our sins. Beloved, if God so loved us, we ought also to love one another.

1 John 4:7–11

When I was serving as a mission president, I once interviewed an elder who said he felt cold inside. He did not feel God's love for him, and he did not feel any love for others. Nor did he have a desire to do the work. Some days he just sat on his bed and did not go out. Because he was so discouraged, his junior companion had decided not to push him too hard, not wanting his senior companion to feel worse than he already did. I encouraged this elder the best I could, and I gave him a blessing.

The next time I saw him, I asked how he was doing. He said he had prayed to God and that God had warmed his heart. He said he had adopted my suggestion to "pray unto the Father with all the energy of heart, that [he might] be filled with this love [charity], which [God] hath bestowed upon all who are true followers of his Son, Jesus Christ" (Moroni 7:48). As a result, this elder felt so much love for others. His hard time and his crisis of faith had passed. He was such a wonderful young man, and I was so happy about the positive turn of events. Charity is an absolutely essential attribute for a missionary—for all of us.

This chapter is about charity and love. Charity is the pure love of Christ (see Moroni 7:47). It is Christlike love. In Chapter 2, I wrote that humility is the foundational attribute. But I think it's abundantly clear that, if you had to pick one attribute that best characterizes God or His Son, that attribute would be charity. God is love (1 John 4:8). And if we are to become like Him, we must be filled with this pure love. We know that faith, hope, and charity are linked. As important as faith and hope are, the greatest of these is charity (see 1 Corinthians 13:13).

And yet, humility, being the foundational attribute, is tied to charity, as we learn from Mormon: "For none is acceptable before God, save the meek and lowly in heart; and if a man be meek and lowly in heart, and confesses by the power of the Holy Ghost that Jesus is the Christ, he must needs have charity; for if he have not charity he is nothing; wherefore he must needs have charity" (Moroni 7:44).

In the Greek language, there are three kinds of love:

1. *Eros*—romantic love.
2. *Philia*—brotherly love, from which we get the name of the city Philadelphia, the city of brotherly love.
3. *Agape*—Godlike love; the ability to love the unlovable; the love of a mother.

This chapter focuses on *agape*—Godlike love.

At this point in our study, a lawyer comes in handy. Thank heavens the lawyer asked the Lord what the great commandment was (yes, I know the lawyer wasn't trying to be helpful). "Then one of them, which was a lawyer, asked him a question, tempting him, and saying, Master, which is the great commandment in the law? Jesus said unto him, Thou shalt love the Lord thy God with all thy heart, and with all thy soul, and with all thy mind. This is the first and great commandment. And the second is like unto it, Thou shalt love thy neighbour as thyself. On these two commandments hang all the law and the prophets" (Matthew 22:35–40).

So, the two great commandments are to love God and to love your neighbor. In Galatians we read: "For all the law is fulfilled in one word, even in this; Thou shalt love thy neighbor as thyself" (Galatians 5:14). (It was more than one word, but that's okay.)

Loving God

How do we show our love for God? Jesus said, "If ye love me, keep my commandments" (John 14:15). John taught: "For this is the love of God, that we keep his commandments" (1 John 5:3). If we love God, we will naturally strive to keep His commandments. When we fall short, as we will, we will feel sad about our failure, and we will implement the steps of repentance. If we love God, we will also be grateful for His many blessings. Our prayers will be filled with "thank thees" as well as petitions. We will want to learn of Him, so we will be dedicated in our scripture study. We will love His gospel and be happy to share it. We will be willing to "stand as witnesses of God at all times and in all things, and in all places" (Mosiah 18:9). We will be dedicated and faithful, always desiring to be in His service. We won't just express our love for God with our mouths; we will express our love by our actions.

Loving Our Neighbor

In exploring how we love our neighbor, the first question is, who is our neighbor? Once again, a lawyer—though not trying to be helpful—helped us solve this question by asking the Master:

> And, behold, a certain lawyer stood up, and tempted him, saying, Master, what shall I do to inherit eternal life? He said unto him, What is written in the law? how readest thou? And he answering said, Thou shalt love the Lord thy God with all thy heart, and with all thy soul, and with all thy strength, and with all thy mind; and thy neighbour as thyself. And he said unto him, Thou hast answered right: this do, and thou shalt live. But he, willing to justify himself, said unto Jesus, And who is my neighbour? And Jesus answering said, A certain man went down from Jerusalem to Jericho, and fell among thieves, which stripped him of his raiment, and wounded him, and departed, leaving him half dead. And by chance there came down a certain priest that way: and when he saw him, he passed by on the other side. And likewise a Levite, when he was at the place, came

> and looked on him, and passed by on the other side. But a certain Samaritan, as he journeyed, came where he was: and when he saw him, he had compassion on him, And went to him, and bound up his wounds, pouring in oil and wine, and set him on his own beast, and brought him to an inn, and took care of him. And on the morrow when he departed, he took out two pence, and gave them to the host, and said unto him, Take care of him; and whatsoever thou spendest more, when I come again, I will repay thee. Which now of these three, thinkest thou, was neighbour unto him that fell among the thieves? And he said, He that shewed mercy on him. Then said Jesus unto him, Go, and do thou likewise. (Luke 10:25–37)

The answer to the question is that everyone is our neighbor. Even our enemies are our neighbors (see Matthew 5:43–44). A woman once criticized Abraham Lincoln for being kind to his enemies. She said that Lincoln should destroy his enemies; instead he was treating them like his friends. Lincoln wisely responded, "Do I not destroy my enemies when I make them my friends?"[1]

I was blessed to have a good example of neighbor-loving at home. My parents were the ultimate modern-day good Samaritans. After their passing, hoping to preserve their memory for future generations, I wrote and compiled a book honoring their lives. Here is part of the introduction to that book:

> To know Rusty and Gloria Rife was to love them.
>
> Those of us who knew them have been greatly blessed by our association with them. Gloria and Rusty were not rich; they were not famous; they did not hold high position. They were not perfect. But they were good, very good. And as they grew older, they just kept getting better (and that's the whole point, isn't it?).
>
> They had a great marriage, an exemplary marriage. They were kind to one another, and they were understanding toward and kind to others. They did many good deeds. They visited the sick, comforted the widow, and loved little children. They attended weddings, funerals, and every other important event in the lives of their family members and friends. They carried with them a spirit of love, acceptance, and good humor. One always felt better in their presence.
>
> Gloria and Rusty understood the difference between worldly possessions and portable things—things we can take with us through the veil. Money was of little importance to them. They did not have much of it, but they were generous with what they had. Relationships

were important to them—family relationships and friendships. Yes, they excelled in the relationship business.

What a blessing it was to learn at the feet of loving and charitable parents! I remember whining as a child about having to stop my childhood game to carry lunch or dinner to our elderly neighbors, the Higbees. But now, I marvel that for several years my lower-middle-class parents, worried that the Higbees might not be eating properly, made an extra plate of lunch and dinner on a daily basis for Mr. and Mrs. Higbee. At the time, Mr. Higbee was a bit delusional and often complained that my dad had stolen this or that from him. Unfazed, my dad would laugh and say, "Oh Bill, you know I didn't take your darn hammer" (only he wouldn't say darn). And then Bill would laugh and agree that my dad would never do such a thing—until the next day, when the conversation was repeated all over again.

It's important to note that we cannot keep the first great commandment (to love God) without keeping the second great commandment (to love our neighbor). "If a man say, I love God, and hateth his brother, he is a liar: for he that loveth not his brother whom he hath seen, how can he love God whom he hath not seen? And this commandment have we from him, That he who loveth God love his brother also" (1 John 4:20–21).

It is also important to consider that the commandment is to love thy neighbor as thyself. We should—we must—love ourselves. This is not inconsistent with humility. A person must love himself or herself before he or she can effectively love others. It helps to know who we are and who we can become. We must be temperate (or patient with ourselves) while at the same time being diligent (or demanding of ourselves).

Jesus Was Love Personified

In a very real way, Jesus was love personified. God's love was manifested through Jesus Christ: "For God so loved the world, that he gave his only begotten Son, that whosoever believeth in him should not perish, but have everlasting life" (John 3:16).

Jesus gave His life for his friends, and "greater love hath no man than this, that a man lay down his life for his friends" (John 15:13). In 1 John we read, "We love him, because he first loved us" (1 John 4:19). The Atonement is the ultimate expression of Jesus' love for us.

Who can forget the tender and loving way He suffered the little children to come to Him, both in the Old and New Worlds? Or the kind way in which He dealt with the woman caught in adultery? President Kimball wrote:

> [Jesus] was beaten, officially scourged. He wore a crown of thorns, a wicked torture. He was mocked and jeered. He suffered every indignity at the hands of his own people. 'I came unto my own,' he said, 'and my own received me not.' He was required to carry his own cross, taken to the mount of Calvary, nailed to a cross, and suffered excruciating pain. Finally, with the soldiers and his accusers down below him, he looked upon the Roman soldiers and said these immortal words: 'Father, forgive them; for they know not what they do.' (Luke 23:34.)[2]

There is no better example of the pure love of Christ than his gracious plea: "Father, forgive them; for they know not what they do." I like a line from the lyrics of a song about Jesus sung by Las Vegas performer Danny Gans, who was a committed Christian. It goes: "Only Love can give Itself so others can go free."[3] Jesus truly did give himself so we could go free.

Why Charity Is Important in Our Lives

Let's look at how important it is that we develop charity in our lives. From 1 Corinthians 13:1–3 (see also Moroni 7:46) we learn:

> Though I speak with the tongues of men and of angels, and have not charity, I am become as sounding brass, or a tinkling cymbal. And though I have the gift of prophecy, and understand all mysteries, and all knowledge; and though I have all faith, so that I could remove mountains, and have not charity, I am nothing. And though I bestow all my goods to feed the poor, and though I give my body to be burned, and have not charity, it profiteth me nothing.

The Prophet Joseph Smith put it this way: "All men's religion is vain without charity."[4] If we give out love and charity, they will be returned to us. As President George Q. Cannon said, "If we have been merciful, kind, sympathetic, *filled with charity and love*, we will have these repaid to us; but if we have not exercised these heavenly qualities, we may depend upon it, unless we have repented and made atonement, they will be measured to us in the same manner that we have measured them to others. God is just, and He cannot even wink at iniquity, much less countenance it."[5]

Charity Further Defined

As taught in 1 Corinthians and Moroni, to have charity involves the following:

- Being long-suffering
- Being kind
- Not being envious
- Not being proud
- Not pursuing one's own interests
- Not being easily provoked
- Thinking no evil
- Rejoicing in truth
- Being full of hope and faith
- Enduring all things

So charity contains within its definition several of the other Godlike characteristics: patience, kindness, humility, temperance, faith, and hope. A charitable person is patient, long-suffering, kind, humble, temperate, and full of faith and hope. A charitable person is not demanding, harsh, or condescending.

Charity is the pure love of Christ; it is Christlike love (see Moroni 7:47). It is the bond of perfectness and peace (see Colossians 3:14; D&C 88:125). President Joseph F. Smith said, "Charity, or love, is the greatest principle in existence. If we can lend a helping hand to the oppressed, if we can aid those who are despondent and in sorrow, if we can uplift and ameliorate the condition of mankind, it is our mission to do it, it is an essential part of our religion to do it."[6]

A person who is full of charity forgives easily and asks for forgiveness humbly. When I was young, there was a popular movie called *Love Story*. At a poignant moment in the plot, the young husband said to his sick wife, "I'm sorry." And she responded, "Don't you know that love means never having to say you're sorry?"[7] I have never heard such a ridiculous statement. Love does mean saying you're sorry. And love also means forgiving and asking for forgiveness.

Benefits of Charity

The benefits of charity (not to mention that we are nothing without it) include the following:

- It will cover a multitude of sins (see 1 Peter 4:8) or, as stated in the Joseph Smith translation, will prevent a multitude of sins.
- It is edifying, for "knowledge puffeth up, but charity edifieth" (1 Corinthians 8:1).
- It is the "bond of perfectness and peace" (D&C 88:125; see also Colossians 3:14).
- It helps us abound in good works, when combined with faith and hope (Alma 7:24).
- It casts out all fear (1 John 4:18; Moroni 8:16).
- It qualifies us for the work (D&C 4:5–6; D&C 12:8).
- It helps us know God (D&C 107:30–31).
- It allows our confidence to wax strong, even in the presence of God (D&C 121:45).

I have known many charitable people, and I'm sure you have too. As I mentioned previously, my parents were full of charity and love. President Kimball was also a good example of charity. President Thomas S. Monson is a man of charity who has a remarkable personal ministry. Think of people you know who are full of charity and ask yourself what you can do to be more like them.

How Can I Develop Charity?

If we ask how we can obtain charity, the answer, in major part, is that charity is a spiritual gift from God. In the end, we can't earn it completely. It must be bestowed upon us (see Moroni 7:48) as it was upon the missionary I spoke of at the beginning of this chapter. Bruce and Marie Hafen wrote: "As we begin to follow Christ, then, the Lord gives us charity—a natural impulse to extend mercy and grace to others as we receive them from him."[8]

President George Q. Cannon emphasized that charity is a gift for which we should pray. "If any of us are imperfect, it is our duty to pray for the gift that will make us perfect. Have I imperfections? I am full of them. What is my duty? To pray to God to give me the gifts that will correct these imperfections. *If I am an angry man, it is my duty to pray for charity, which suffereth long and is kind.* Am I an envious man? *It is my duty to seek for charity, which envieth not.* So with all the gifts of the Gospel. They are intended for this purpose."[9]

C. S. Lewis taught the same principle in a very memorable way:

> *When I come to my evening prayers and try to reckon up the sins of the day, nine times out of ten the most obvious one is some sin against charity*; I have sulked or snapped or sneered or snubbed or stormed. And the excuse that immediately springs to my mind is that the provocation was so sudden and unexpected: I was caught off my guard, I had not time to collect myself. . . . Surely what a man does when he is taken off his guard is the best evidence for what sort of man he is? Surely what pops out before the man has time to put on a disguise is the truth? If there are rats in the cellar you are most likely to see them if you go in very suddenly. But the suddenness does not create the rats: it only prevents them from hiding. In the same way the suddenness of the provocation does not make me an ill-tempered man: it only shows me what an ill-tempered man I am. . . . Now that cellar is out of reach of my conscious will. I can to some extent control my acts: I have no direct control over my temperament. And if (as I said before) what we are matters even more than what we do—if indeed, what we do matters chiefly as evidence of what we are—then it follows that the change which I most need to undergo is a change that my own direct, voluntary efforts cannot bring about. . . . But I cannot, by direct moral effort, give myself new motives. *After the first few steps in the Christian life we realise that everything which really needs to be done in our souls can be done only by God.*[10]

According to the *Encyclopedia of Mormonism*, obtaining the Christ-like virtues, including charity, involves an interactive relationship between human and divine powers. In other words, we must try, and God must help. "Individuals lack the capacity to develop a Christlike nature by their own effort. The perfecting attributes such as hope and charity are ultimately 'bestowed upon all who are true followers . . . of Jesus Christ' (Moroni 7:48) by grace through his Atonement."[11] Even so, I do not believe God will bestow the gift of charity upon us if we are not praying for it and trying our best to manifest this pure love.

We Need to Develop Charity in Our Lives

When the Lord appears, we will need to be like Him (see Moroni

7:48). And since He is love, that means we must also be full of love.

Joseph Smith taught, "Love is one of the chief characteristics of Deity, and ought to be manifested by those who aspire to be the sons of God. A man filled with the love of God is not content with blessing his family alone, but ranges through the whole world, anxious to bless the whole human race."[12] In this quote, the Prophet Joseph spoke of "a man filled with the love of God." But when it comes to charity, we men have much to learn from our sisters in the gospel. As President Kimball said, "Women display a remarkable capacity to love and to cope, along with a remarkable empathy for others in difficulty, which moves women to service as they express their goodness quietly. Women, so often, are charity personified."[13]

God has commanded us to have charity and has said that if we do not have charity we are nothing (see 2 Nephi 26:30). In fact, "the end of the commandment is charity" (1 Timothy 1:5). We are to do all things with charity (1 Corinthians 16:14). And whoso is found possessed of charity at the last day, it will be well with him (see Moroni 7:47). That's true whether it's the last day of the earth or, more likely, our last day on the earth. Unless we have charity, we cannot inherit the place that the Lord has prepared for us in the mansions of His Father (see Ether 12:34; Moroni 10:21).

May we all pray for this most important gift of the Spirit and then make our best efforts to be full of charity and love.

Summary

- Charity is the pure love of Christ. It is the greatest of the divine attributes, for God is love.
- Humility is helpful in developing charity.
- The two great commandments are to love God and to love others as ourselves. We cannot keep the first great commandment without keeping the second.
- We need to love ourselves or we cannot fully love others.
- Jesus is the most magnificent example of charity and love. Other mortals have set, and continue to set, good examples of charity.
- Our religion is vain without charity.
- If we live a life of charity and love, we will have charity and love repaid to us.

- Charity includes within its scriptural definition many of the other Christlike attributes.
- A person who has charity forgives easily and asks for forgiveness humbly.
- Charity is a gift; we must pray for it and then attempt to develop it in our life.
- Women are often charity personified.
- If we are found with charity at the last day, it will be well with us.

Notes

1. Alex Ayres, *The Wit and Wisdom of Abraham Lincoln* (New York: Penguin Books, 1992), 71.
2. Kimball, *The Miracle of Forgiveness*, 280.
3. Danny Gans, *Brand New Dream*, "Those Simple Words You Said" (Sony, February 29, 2000), track 5.
4. Joseph Smith, *History of The Church of Jesus Christ of Latter-day Saints*, vol. 1, with introduction and notes by B. H. Roberts (Salt Lake City: The Church of Jesus Christ of Latter-day Saints, 1932–51), 275.
5. George Q. Cannon, *Gospel Truth: Discourses and Writings of President George Q. Cannon*, vol. 1, ed. Jerreld L. Newquist (Salt Lake City: Deseret Book, 1974), 163, emphasis added.
6. Joseph F. Smith in Conference Report, April 1917, 4.
7. Erich Segal, *Love Story* (Hollywood: Paramount, 1970).
8. Bruce C. Hafen and Marie K. Hafen, *The Belonging Heart: The Atonement and Relationships with God and Family* (Salt Lake City: Deseret Book, 1994), 17.
9. George Q. Cannon, as quoted in Robert L. Millet, *Steadfast and Immovable: Striving for Spiritual Maturity* (Salt Lake City: Deseret Book, 1992), 99, emphasis added.
10. C. S. Lewis, *Mere Christianity* (New York: HarperOne, 1952) 192–93, emphasis added.
11. *Encyclopedia of Mormonism*, 562.
12. Joseph Smith, *Discourses of the Prophet Joseph Smith*, comp. Alma P. Burton (Salt Lake City: Deseret Book, 1997), 205.
13. Spencer W. Kimball, *My Beloved Sisters* (Salt Lake City: Deseret Book, 1979), 20.

6

Patience and Long-suffering

And now I would that ye should be humble, and be submissive and gentle; easy to be entreated; full of patience and long-suffering; being temperate in all things; being diligent in keeping the commandments of God at all times; asking for whatsoever things ye stand in need, both spiritual and temporal; always returning thanks unto God for whatsoever things ye do receive.

Alma 7:23

In your patience possess ye your souls.

Luke 21:19; see also D&C 101:38

One day, a new missionary in the Korea Daejeon Mission called to tell me he wanted to transfer to another mission. Korean is one of the hardest languages in the world. It takes many months to become even marginally proficient. This elder felt that it was a waste of valuable mission time to follow his senior companion around like a "whipped puppy" for half of his mission. He wanted to be transferred to an English-speaking mission where he thought he would be able to make better use of his full twenty-four months.

Although he was serving in a faraway city, I asked the elder to come to the mission office the following day so I could speak with him in person. For the rest of the day, I thought of nothing else. In the middle of the night, I awakened with six or seven thoughts to share with my elder to persuade him that his mission assignment was divinely inspired and that he should stay with us and complete his mission in Korea. I dutifully wrote down this inspiration in the night so I wouldn't forget it in the morning.

The following day, I met with this elder. Our meeting lasted for many hours. I tried all the spiritually motivated reasons I had thought of for why he should stay. He was kind and polite but determined to serve in an English-speaking mission. Finally, in near frustration, I said, "Elder, do you know how hard it is to change a mission call? I'll have to talk with our area president (a General Authority); he will call the missionary department; the missionary department will call your stake president; your stake president and bishop will talk with your parents. Your parents will call you on the telephone to try to persuade you to stay in Korea. If that fails, your stake president will call you. If that fails, someone from the missionary department will call you. If he fails, then I will need to talk with you again. And if I'm not successful, then a General Authority will speak with you. Even then, I'm not sure your wish will be granted to change missions."

That was my last argument. It was not a very spiritual argument. It was more of a logistical argument, after all my spiritual attempts had failed. The elder paused for a moment and then said, rather casually, "Okay, I'll stay." We shook hands, we hugged, and he left my office. My assistants reported that before returning to his area, he purchased several Korean language books from the office missionaries.

Over the ensuing months, this great elder, a brilliant young man, studied diligently and learned Korean better and faster than most of our missionaries. He later served as an assistant to the president. At first, our elder had little patience for studying the second hardest language in the world for an English speaker to learn. But once he made up his mind, he studied patiently until he learned the language and became an exemplary missionary. He fulfilled his mission assignment with honor and distinction.

It took patience for our missionary (and now dear friend) to perform his mission. It will take the Godlike attribute of patience for you to fulfill your life's mission, whatever that may be. Your life mission is likely to last much longer than two years. Therefore you will need to "run with patience the race that is set before [you]" (Hebrews 12:1).

Patience and Long-suffering Defined

The dictionary definitions of "patience" include the following:

- Bearing provocation, annoyance, misfortune, or pain, without complaint, loss of temper, irritation, or the like
- An ability or willingness to suppress restlessness or annoyance when confronted with delay
- Quiet, steady perseverance
- Even-tempered care

Similarly "diligence" is defined as "to work with patience."[1] The dictionary definitions of long-suffering are:

- The quality of enduring injury, trouble, or provocation long and patiently
- Patient endurance
- The quality of being not easily provoked[2]

These definitions refer to a world of trouble—provocation, annoyance, delay, misfortune, and pain. The scriptures also speak often about being patient in afflictions, tribulation, suffering, and persecution. (See 1 Peter 2:20; D&C 98:2; Romans 12:12; Alma 17:11; Alma 20:29; Alma 26:28; D&C 24:8; D&C 31:9; D&C 54:10; Alma 34:40–41; D&C 66:9.)

I suppose when Joseph Smith walked out of the Sacred Grove after having experienced the First Vision, he had no idea of the persecution and troubles that lay ahead for him, his family, and his followers. But in 1830, the Lord said to Joseph Smith: "Be patient in afflictions; for thou shalt have many" (D&C 24:8). While Joseph had more than his fair share of afflictions, there is no doubt that we all will have plenty of them as we navigate our way through this second estate. President Kimball taught, "Being human, we would expel from our lives sorrow, distress, physical pain, and mental anguish and assure ourselves of continual ease and comfort. But if we closed the doors upon such, we might be evicting our greatest friends and benefactors. Suffering can make saints of people as they learn *patience, long-suffering*, and self-mastery. The sufferings of our Savior were part of his education."[3]

Suffering can help make us saints as we learn patience and long-suffering. If suffering was part of the Savior's education, suffering patiently will be an important part of our mortal education as well. It will prepare our souls for eternity. But it will also help us be better people here and now, people who can empathize with, comfort, and encourage others.

Patience goes beyond enduring the major afflictions. We need to learn patience even in the minor irritations of life. President George Q. Cannon said: "It is a precious gift to have the gift of patience, to be good-tempered, to be cheerful, to not be depressed, to not give way to wrong feelings and become impatient and irritable. It is a blessed gift for all to possess."[4] We are told to seek after the best gifts, and we can seek after the gift of patience.

Is patience a gift? As we know from previous chapters, all the divine virtues are gifts, in a sense, for we need to pray to God to change our hearts and help us develop them. But, we also know that we must make efforts on our on part to be patient and long-suffering in the face of major trials or minor irritations.

In developing patience, we need to be patient with ourselves. The second great commandment is to love others as we love ourselves—meaning loving yourself is part of the commandment. Similarly, the commandment to be patient must also apply to being patient with yourself. It's certainly a trick to balance the seemingly opposing commandments to be diligent and to be patient. We need to try hard; we need to expect a lot of ourselves; but we also need to give ourselves a break. Balance is hard to find, but we need to seek for it.

As I was writing this chapter, my dear wife, Janet, had an experience at Walmart, where she went to buy paint. A new trainee was learning how to mix paint. Along with a more experienced worker, he tried twice to mix the right blue color without success. Finally, after more than twenty minutes, the manager had to come and get it right on the third time. Janet remarked to me that had she been a young mother with small children in tow, she would have been upset, irritated, and impatient with the delay and incompetent service. But Janet said, "One of the benefits of being our age is that we can relax, take a deep breath, and wait patiently in such times of minor irritations." Janet's waiting patiently, rather than getting upset, made life a little better that day for a new trainee at Walmart too. Patience includes elements of love and kindness.

The Apostle Paul spoke of this doctrine: "That the aged men be sober, grave, temperate, sound in faith, in charity, in patience" (Titus 2:2). Having a little age and experience under our belts helps all of us, men or women, be "sound in patience." If you're young and feisty, don't give up. Don't be discouraged; keep trying. You can learn to be patient and long-suffering over time. (It will really help if you don't have crying children in your shopping cart.)

We need to keep at it, though. Patience is a key to taking upon ourselves the divine nature over time. We are to "continue in patience until [we] are perfected" (D&C 67:13). We are to "let patience have her perfect work, that [we] may be perfect and entire, wanting nothing" (James 1:4).

The Patience and Long-suffering of the Father and the Son

God the Father and His Son, Jesus Christ, are full of patience and long-suffering. I know this from Their interactions with me, as They patiently bear with my sins and weaknesses. And I know this from my study of the scriptures.

In Mosiah, "If ye have come to a knowledge of the goodness of God, and his matchless power, and his wisdom, and his patience, and his long-suffering towards the children of men" (Mosiah 4:6). And in Alma, "And not many days hence the Son of God shall come in his glory; and his glory shall be the glory of the Only Begotten of the Father, full of grace, equity, and truth, full of patience, mercy, and long-suffering, quick to hear the cries of his people and to answer their prayers" (Alma 9:26).

The New Testament tells us, "The Lord is not slack concerning his promise, as some men count slackness; but is longsuffering toward us, not willing that any should perish, but that all should come to repentance" (2 Peter 3:9).

Returning to Alma, we read, "Therefore, let us glory, yea, we will glory in the Lord; yea, we will rejoice, for our joy is full; yea, we will praise our God forever. Behold, who can glory too much in the Lord? Yea, who can say too much of his great power, and of his mercy, and of his long-suffering towards the children of men? Behold, I say unto you, I cannot say the smallest part which I feel" (Alma 26:16).

And finally, "My son, be faithful in Christ; and may not the things which I have written grieve thee, to weigh thee down unto death; but may Christ lift thee up, and may his sufferings and death, and the showing his body unto our fathers, and his mercy and long-suffering, and the hope of his glory and of eternal life, rest in your mind forever" (Moroni 9:25).

There are many other scriptures that speak of God's patience (see Exodus 34:6; Numbers 14:18; Psalms 86:15; Mormon 2:12). We are told to retain in remembrance the Lord's mercy and long-suffering (Alma 5:6; see also Moroni 9:25).

I confess that the Old Testament is not my favorite book of scripture. I'm sure this says more about me than it does about the Old Testament. Before you judge me too harshly, though, keep in mind that I have read it in its entirety. My wife once taught me a great lesson about the Old Testament. Like me, she has sometimes wondered what the point of the Old Testament is. Of course, we know that the Old Testament is deep in meaning and rich in symbolism. But it dawned on my wife that one main message of the Old Testament is that God doesn't give up on us. How many times did the Old Testament people let Him down and fall away? And how many times did the Lord patiently forgive them and give them another chance? Many, many times.

This is also the message of Jacob 5, the allegory of the olive tree. God is exceedingly patient and long-suffering with us, His children, and is willing to forgive us if we seek Him in humility and sincerity.

I have a list of scriptures I like to read sometimes while taking the sacrament. These verses help me remember the Savior's sacrifice for me. Here is one of them: "And the world, because of their iniquity, shall judge him to be a thing of naught; wherefore they scourge him, and he suffereth it; and they smite him, and he suffereth it. Yea, they spit upon him, and he suffereth it, because of his loving kindness and his long-suffering towards the children of men" (1 Nephi 19:9). As this scripture indicates, there is a connection between mercy and kindness, on the one hand, and patience and long-suffering, on the other. It is much easier and requires much less effort to be patient and long-suffering if we also happen to be full of loving kindness and mercy. God's patience with us, His children, flows naturally from His loving kindness and mercy.

Mere Mortals

Now let's look at some examples of mere mortals who developed the qualities of patience and long-suffering. We would be wrong not to start with a man who had the patience of Job. I refer, of course, to Job himself. President Monson wrote,

> Job was a "perfect and upright" man who "feared God, and eschewed evil." (Job 1:1) Pious in his conduct, prosperous in his fortune, Job was to face a test which could have destroyed anyone. Shorn of his possessions, scorned by his friends, afflicted by his suffering, shattered by the loss of his family, he was urged to "curse God, and die." (Job 2:9) He resisted this temptation and declared from the depths of his noble soul, "Behold, my witness is in heaven, and my record is on high." (Job 16:19) "I know that my redeemer liveth." (Job 19:25)
>
> Job became a model of unlimited patience. To this day we refer to those who are long-suffering as having the patience of Job. He provides an example for us to follow.[5]

Job was able to overcome all his trials because he knew his Redeemer lived. Having strong and vibrant faith in the Lord Jesus Christ will naturally help us become more patient and long-suffering.

I have read many biographies of Abraham Lincoln, who was patient and self-disciplined. In his later years, he was remarkably slow to anger. He was described as a "forbearing man who, as president, cultivated his adversaries, appointed his opponents to responsible positions, and refused to engage in or take offense at personal abuse."[6] The prophet Abraham was also patient, for as Paul wrote: "And so, after he [Abraham] had patiently endured, he obtained the promise" (Hebrews 6:15).

I'm sure you know people who are patient and long-suffering. I home teach Richard and Donae Lewis. Donae has rheumatoid arthritis and is confined to a wheelchair. She has had many operations and health problems in the past few years and suffers constant pain, yet Donae has a perpetual smile on her face and a love for the Lord and for His gospel. Richard cheerfully cares for her, in addition to working full time. There is no one for whom he has greater admiration or love. The angelic sisters of our Relief Society visit Donae every weekday at 1:00 PM and 5:00 PM to help her. Donae is blessed by their loving assistance, and they are blessed by Donae's faithful and grateful spirit. With Richard's support,

Donae is active in every ward meeting and event. Donae and Richard are excellent examples to me of saints who are patient and long-suffering. I recently told Donae that when I die, the first thing I'll do is look around for her. If I see her, I'll know I'm in the right place; if I don't see her, I'll start to worry. (This all assumes I can outlive her.)

Once when I was preparing a talk, I thought about asking why we had to *endure* to the end; why couldn't we *rejoice* to the end? Enduring sounds like a real downer. For me, mortality isn't so bad. I was sure I could rejoice to the end, instead of just enduring. But then I thought of Donae in her wheelchair. For her, it really is a matter of enduring, rather than rejoicing, to the end. And yet, she endures cheerfully, which is amazing and awe-inspiring.

In Olympic diving terms, my life is about as difficult as doing a cannonball, while Donae's degree of difficulty is that of doing a "backward two-and-a-half somersaults with two-and-a-half twists in the piked position" (generally known as the hardest dive). It is clear, though, that for all of us, even if our life's "degree of difficulty" is less than Donae's, enduring to the end of mortal probation will require substantial patience and long-suffering. But it is also clear that enduring will lead to happiness. "Take, my brethren, the prophets, who have spoken in the name of the Lord, for an example of suffering affliction, and of patience. *Behold we count them happy which endure*. Ye have heard of the patience of Job, and have seen the end of the Lord; that the Lord is very pitiful, and of tender mercy" (James 5:10–11, emphasis added).

The scriptures teach us the many ways and the many circumstances in which we need to be patient and long-suffering. The following scriptures are in addition to the numerous scriptures already cited about being patient in afflictions and trials.

- We must be patient as we wait for the coming of the Lord (see James 5:7–8; Psalm 37:7; 2 Thessalonians 3:5)
- We must wait patiently on the Lord in other matters (D&C 98:2; see also D&C 108:4).
- We must be patient toward all men (1 Thessalonians 5:14).
- We should receive the word of the Lord from the Prophet "in all patience and faith" (D&C 21:5).
- We must be patient in the development and nurturing of faith (see Alma 32:41–43; Luke 8:15).

The Apostle Paul taught that bishops are to be patient (see 1 Timothy 3:3). This is also true of ministers, men of God, servants of the Lord, and all Saints (see 2 Timothy 2:24; 2 Corinthians 6:4; 1 Timothy 6:11; Mosiah 3:19). The decisions of the leading quorums of the Church are to be made in patience (see D&C 107:30). My favorite passage of scripture is Section 121 of the Doctrine and Covenants, which teaches how the priesthood is to be exercised. In the world, persons in authority generally give orders and their subordinates obey, whether they want to or not. But that is not how the priesthood is supposed to work. "No power or influence can or ought to be maintained by virtue of the priesthood, only by persuasion, *by long-suffering*, by gentleness and meekness, and by love unfeigned; By kindness, and pure knowledge, which shall greatly enlarge the soul without hypocrisy, and without guile" (D&C 121:41–42, emphasis added).

A priesthood leader is to lead by persuasion, not dictatorially. A priesthood leader invites, suggests, and encourages; he does not order people around. He is to be long-suffering, gentle, meek, and genuinely loving. His ministry should be one of kindness, without any hypocrisy or guile. This is the definition of a servant-leader; this is a description of how Jesus leads.

I have long believed that the principles of priesthood leadership taught in Section 121 of the Doctrine and Covenants apply equally to our roles as mothers and fathers. In the end, we need to persuade and gently and lovingly lead our children—we cannot force them. We need to "reprove [them] betimes with sharpness, when moved upon by the Holy Ghost," but we also need to "[show] forth afterwards an increase of love" (D&C 121:43). If our "dominion," or family, is to be "an everlasting dominion," it will need to flow unto us "without compulsory means" (see D&C 121:46).

We have ample evidence from the scriptures that missionaries need patience and long-suffering. We should warn our sons and daughters of this before sending them out in the world. This was the counsel the Lord gave the sons of Mosiah as they went to preach to the Lamanites: "And the Lord said unto them also: Go forth among the Lamanites, thy brethren, and establish my word; *yet ye shall be patient in long-suffering and afflictions*, that ye may show forth good example unto them in me, and I will make an instrument of thee in my hands unto the salvation of many souls" (Alma 17:11, emphasis added).

Ammon later had to rescue his brethren in Middoni, with the help of Lamoni, "And when Ammon did meet them he was exceedingly sorrowful, for behold they were naked, and their skins were worn exceedingly because of being bound with strong cords. And they also had suffered hunger, thirst, and all kinds of afflictions; *nevertheless they were patient in all their sufferings*" (Alma 20:29, emphasis added).

Alma spoke of his missionary labors as follows:

> Now when our hearts were depressed, and we were about to turn back, behold, the Lord comforted us, and said: Go amongst thy brethren, the Lamanites, and *bear with patience thine afflictions*, and I will give unto you success. And now behold, we have come, and been forth amongst them; and *we have been patient in our sufferings*, and we have suffered every privation; yea, we have traveled from house to house, relying upon the mercies of the world—not upon the mercies of the world alone but upon the mercies of God. (Alma 26:27–28, emphasis added)

Patience is undoubtedly a missionary virtue (see D&C 4:6). Alma was proud of his missionary son Shiblon for his patience and long-suffering among the people of the Zoramites (see Alma 38:3). And, as I began this chapter with a less dramatic example, it took my young missionary (and all the rest of us missionaries who served in Korea) a significant amount of time and patience to learn the Korean language so we could share the gospel in that wonderful country.

How to Develop Patience and Long-suffering

It takes time to develop patience. As my wife learned, it's easier to be patient as you get older. It's also easier to be patient if you're full of love, kindness, and mercy. When we're in a tough situation, things tend to get better if we just hang in there. Or, as stated in Ecclesiastes, "Better is the end of a thing than the beginning thereof: and the patient in spirit is better than the proud in spirit" (Ecclesiastes 7:8).

We can and should pray for patience: "But that ye would humble yourselves before the Lord, and call on his holy name, and watch and pray continually, that ye may not be tempted above that which ye can bear, and thus be led by the Holy Spirit, becoming humble, meek, submissive, patient, full of love and all long-suffering" (Alma 13:28). Being long-suffering is one of the fruits of the Spirit (see Galatians

5:22). As we have the Spirit guiding us in our lives, we will naturally become more patient and long-suffering.

We can practice being patient in small things. When we confront an irritating, annoying situation, we can recognize it as an opportunity to develop patience. We can "suppress annoyance" when confronted with delay, such as my wife did in Walmart. We can wait patiently for someone to exit the crowded parking lot ahead of us. We can try to be more patient with our family members and ward members. One blessing of being active in the Church is the opportunity to bump up against, interact with, forgive, lift, and strengthen other people who may or may not be like us. We are to be "longsuffering" toward our fellow Saints, "forbearing one another in love" (Ephesians 4:2; see also Colossians 3:12–13). We can learn to be generous in judging others and quick to forgive their faults. All of these things will help us grow in patience and long-suffering so we can better handle the greater challenges that are sure to come along.

Sometimes our impatience stems from the inability to get everything done. There is surely more to do than there is time enough to do it. One of our modern-day apostles, Elder Russell M. Nelson, wisely taught that "when priorities are in place, one can more patiently tolerate unfinished business."[7] We can put our priorities in place and then just do the best we can, thus being patient with ourselves.

Conclusion

The Lord has asked us to redouble our diligence, perseverance, patience, and works—and He has promised that if we do so we will in nowise lose our reward (see D&C 127:4). I think we can redouble our patience if we try. This life is more a marathon than it is a sprint. "Let us run with patience the race that is set before us" (Hebrews 12:1).

Summary

- Patience means bearing provocation, annoyance, misfortune, or pain, without complaint, loss of temper, or the like.
- Long-suffering means enduring injury, trouble, or provocation long and patiently.
- When Joseph Smith walked out of the Sacred Grove, he could not have foreseen the persecution and trials that lay before him. Yet, he

and other prophets have been great examples of enduring patiently.

- Trials can help make us saints as we learn patience and long-suffering. We need to learn to be patient in major trials as well as in minor afflictions.
- In a sense, patience can be a spiritual gift, and we should ask God to help us be patient.
- In developing patience, we first must be patient with ourselves. Being patient with ourselves and diligent at the same time is a balancing act.
- Patience has elements of love and kindness.
- It is easier to be patient as we grow older, but we need to try to be patient no matter what our age.
- God and Jesus are full of patience and long-suffering.
- There is a connection between mercy and kindness on the one hand and patience and long-suffering on the other. It is easier to be patient with others when we are full of mercy and kindness.
- There are many examples of mortals who have shown patience and long-suffering, including Job, Abraham, Abraham Lincoln, and some of our friends and neighbors.
- Priesthood leaders need to lead with patience and long-suffering. This same principle applies to parents and missionaries.
- It takes time to develop patience. Sometimes we just need to "hang in there." We should pray for patience and practice it in small things. Having correct priorities can help us press forward patiently.

Notes

1. "Patience," http://dictionary.reference.com/browse/patience
2. "Long-suffering," http://dictionary.reference.com/browse/long-suffering
3. Spencer W. Kimball, *Teachings of Spencer W. Kimball* (Salt Lake City: Bookcraft, 1982), 167, emphasis added.
4. Cannon, *Gospel Truth*, vol. 1, 198.
5. Thomas S. Monson, "Models to Follow," *Ensign*, Nov. 2002, 60.
6. Douglas Wilson, *Lincoln's Sword: The Presidency and the Power of Words* (New York: Vintage, 2006), 26–27.
7. Russell M. Nelson, "Lessons from Eve," *Ensign*, Nov. 1987, 86.

7

Temperance

The Lord is merciful and gracious, slow to anger, and plenteous in mercy.

Psalm 103:8

But speak thou the things which become sound doctrine: That the aged men be sober, grave, temperate, sound in faith, in charity, in patience.

Titus 2:1–2

It might be hard to believe if you looked at me today, but when I was young, I was an athlete. I was especially good at baseball and played on a Church softball team and the high school baseball team. I was also on the high school golf team.

When I was seventeen years old, two events happened in the same week that caused me to realize I had a real weak point. I was playing a practice round of golf at the Hobblecreek Golf Course in Springville, Utah. I teed off on a long par-5 hole. The creek ran just in front of the green. With a long tee shot, and a well played second shot, it was possible to reach the green in two shots and have a chance at an eagle and a good chance at a birdie.

I hit a great tee shot. And then I hit a great second shot—just three feet from the hole. I was sure I would get an easy eagle. I took a good look at the putt and then struck the ball; it hit the corner of the hole and went around and around—and then stayed out of the hole. I was so upset that I threw my putter as high and far in the air as I could, and I yelled out the Lord's name in vain. In my intense anger, I broke the third of the Ten Commandments.

The same week I was playing in a Church fast-pitch softball game. It was the last inning, and my team was at bat. There were two men out and two men on base. We were behind by one run. A teammate was batting, and I was on deck. I was sure that if my teammate got on base, I could get a hit and win the game for our team. The count was full, and the pitcher threw a pitch that was literally a foot over the head of the batter. He did not swing at the pitch. It was clearly ball four; we all knew it. But the umpire yelled out, "Strike three! You're out. Game over." I could not believe it. No one could believe it. It was the worst call I—or anyone else—had ever seen. I was furious. I flung my bat at the umpire so it would bounce just in front of his feet and hit him in the shins. It had the intended effect, but a melee followed.

That night after I returned home from the softball game, I went to my room and did some serious thinking. Within the past week, I had taken the Lord's name in vain because I had missed a three-foot putt in a practice round of golf, and I had inflicted injury on a volunteer umpire in a Church game because he had made a bad call in a game that really didn't matter anyway. It became clear to me, even in my teenage years, that I had a serious problem with my temper. I became angry too easily—even at things that did not matter. I was embarrassed and sad about this. And I felt humble and weak.

As I sat pondering in my room, I read the following scripture from the Book of Mormon: "And if men come unto me I will show unto them their weakness. I give unto men weakness that they may be humble; and my grace is sufficient for all men that humble themselves before me; for if they humble themselves before me, and have faith in me, then will I make weak things become strong unto them" (Ether 12:27). This is the same formula I wrote about in Chapter 4.

Humility + Faith = Strength.

I told God in prayer that I had a weak point—my temper—and I asked for His help. I asked Him for self-control, which I did not know at the time is another term for temperance. And I promised Him that

I would try to control myself better in the future. I had faith that God would help me.

God did help me. He gave me more temperance. But it took effort on my part too. I played many more baseball, basketball, and golf games after that. The umpire or referee missed many calls, and I missed many putts. Sometimes I was in situations when all the other members of my team were angry. A number of times I had to turn around and walk the other way so I would not get involved in the argument. I had to remind myself, over and over, *This is only a game; it doesn't really matter.*

Over time, I learned to be temperate and self-controlled while still being involved in sporting events. I learned to be a good sport. And because I learned to have better self-control in sports, I found that I could do it in life as well. Over time, with God's help and my sincere personal effort, my weakness became my strength—as promised in Ether 12:27: Humility + Faith = Strength.

Don't get me wrong; in the past thirty-five years, I have been known to get angry. But as Janet says about me, "Rich has a very long fuse." It now takes a lot to get me angry, and I attribute this to God's fulfillment of His promise in Ether 12:27.

Before proceeding with this chapter on temperance, let me take a brief aside. Indulge me for just a moment. It is true that we all have our weak points. But I'll tell you something that bothers me (not enough to make me angry, though, because of my temperance). I don't like when people say, referring to their weak points, "That's just the way I am." They usually say this to indicate they are not interested in changing. But, to meet God, to be in His presence, to live in His kingdom, we must be in the process of growing to be like Him. We cannot excuse our faults and weaknesses by saying, "That's just the way I am." We cannot rationalize. We must try to correct our faults—with God's help. And that's what this book is all about.

Temperance Defined

Now, back to temperance. The word *temperate* means moderate or self-restrained; not extreme in opinion or statement; moderate in regard to indulgence of appetites or passions; and modest, forbearing, self-restrained, and not extreme in behavior. Another related word is self-control. A temperate person has self-control in all areas of life.

This book is about striving to take upon ourselves the divine nature. Temperance is one of the virtues comprising the divine nature as described by the Apostle Peter (2 Peter 1:6). The Apostle Paul taught: "And every man that striveth for the mastery is temperate in all things. Now they do it to obtain a corruptible crown; but we an incorruptible" (1 Corinthians 9:25).

President Ezra Taft Benson said, "[An] attribute described by Peter as being part of the divine nature is *temperance*. A priesthood holder is *temperate*. This means he is *restrained* in his emotions and verbal expressions. He does things in *moderation* and is not given to overindulgence. In a word, he has *self-control*. He is the master of his emotions, not the other way around."[1]

Being restrained in "emotions and verbal expressions" means not taking the Lord's name in vain; it means watching what you say and not using profanity. It means not getting angry easily. It means not being "easily provoked" (see 1 Corinthians 13:5). The Apostle Paul taught that a bishop must be "temperate" and "not soon angry" (Titus 1:7–8).

Having served as a bishop three times now for a total of over eleven years, I can testify that being temperate and not soon angry are critically important. Once, more than twenty years ago, I released an adult sister from serving in Young Women and called her to serve in the Primary with the eleven-year-old girls. To my surprise, this sister cried uncontrollably. I didn't know what to do, so I said, "It's obvious that you have loved your calling and have done a great job with the Young Women. I know you will love serving with the eleven-year-old girls, and they will love you too."

Strangely, what this sister thought she heard me say was, "Stop crying; you look ugly when you cry." I know this because she systematically told almost every member of our ward that I had said this to her. "Can you imagine," she said, "a Church leader being so cruel?" My instinct was to go one by one to everyone she had spoken to and tell them it was not true. I had never said such a thing. I had never thought such a thing. It was not within my character even to think such a thing.

So what did I do? After some serious soul-searching at home, I did nothing; I said nothing. I bore the burden of the false accusation, because I felt, upon calm reflection, that I could bear this wrong more easily than I could bear hurting this sister in her obviously delicate emotional state. Many of the members later said to me privately, without my having raised the subject, "I didn't believe it because it didn't sound like you." I hadn't needed to defend myself anyway. After all these years, I am so glad I was not angry too quickly and was able to control my response. It seems that I never regret being too kind, but I always regret being too harsh.

Temperance is one of the fruits of the Spirit (see Galatians 5:22–23). Elder Robert D. Hales stated that the gifts of the Spirit give rise to other gifts, including "the gift to be calm, which includes the ability to curb anger and to be temperate rather than contentious."[2] President David O. McKay once said, "A man who cannot control his temper is not very likely to control his passion, and no matter what his pretensions in religion, he moves in daily life very close to the animal plane."[3]

Being temperate means being moderate and self-disciplined in indulging appetites and passions. I cannot think of anything more important in our twenty-first century world. If we develop the Godlike attribute of temperance, we can avoid the problems that come with such things as unbridled anger, pornography, immorality, drug abuse, overeating, and wasting time.

Curbing Anger

I have already written of the importance of curbing anger. A temperate man is able to avoid the "road rage" so common in our modern world. A temperate person is a peacemaker in the home, not allowing his or her anger to cause hard feelings and sadness. President Ezra Taft Benson wrote, "A priesthood holder who would curse his wife, abuse her with words or actions, or do the same to one of his own children is guilty of grievous sin. 'Can ye be angry, and not sin?' asked the Apostle Paul" (see JST, Eph. 4:26).[4]

The Apostle James wrote, "Wherefore, my beloved brethren, let every man be swift to hear, slow to speak, *slow to wrath*: for the wrath of man worketh not the righteousness of God" (James 1:19–20, emphasis added).

Avoiding Pornography

Temperance means self-control. A man with self-control can discipline himself so he doesn't view pornography. The best approach is never to look at it. It's so tempting, though, just to make a few keystrokes. Pornography is harmful and should be shunned like the plague. Looking at pornography is desensitizing, soul-numbing, and addictive. Typically done secretly, it drives away the Spirit and diminishes self-respect. The viewer, usually a man, progressively requires more depraved acts to view in photographs and videos. He often wants to introduce acts into his marriage that his tender wife finds repugnant and personally offensive. Pornography often leads to adultery, destroying marriages and families and causing much heartbreak.

When serving as a BYU bishop, I received a call one evening from a sister in another state. She told me the sad tale of her husband's addiction to pornography, which led to his unfaithfulness. She told me her daughter, a BYU student in my ward, knew nothing of the situation. She asked me if I would kindly comfort her daughter, as she intended to call her and tell her the shocking news of her father's infidelity and the impending divorce. As she explained the situation to me, asking for my help, she had to stop many times because she was weeping. Think of the magnitude of the combined suffering of all the sisters who have had their tender hearts broken by infidelity that began with pornography.

Pornography addiction can be overcome. The Church is having great success with a wonderful adapted version of the 12-step program. In combination with the Atonement, the 12-step program can help the addict overcome his addiction to pornography, "bridle all [his] passions" (Alma 38:12), regain his self-esteem and the respect of his wife, and muster the temperance necessary to show proper self-control.

Avoiding Drug Abuse

My own family has been impacted by the evil of drug abuse. I won't go into detail, but drug abuse stole twelve years of our precious son's life before he was able to obtain better control. It put a real strain on the rest of us, his family members. It's still a daily struggle, but at the time of this writing, he is doing well. Still, he missed out on many choice experiences in his adolescence and young adulthood, and other people missed out on the service this choice young man could have performed had he not be enslaved by drugs.

While not as devastating as drug addiction, overeating and lack of discipline in diet and exercise result in major health problems. We can abstain from alcohol or drugs, but we cannot abstain from food—and thus it requires temperance to eat sensibly and get enough exercise.

Using Time Wisely

And then there is time-wasting. We all need recreation, and in proper proportions, recreation is good. Family recreation is a great way to build close relationships. Even though "all work and no play make Jack a dull boy," "all play and no work" is not a good formula for success or happiness. Video games may be a good diversion if played sparingly, but they appear to have an addictive effect.

When I was a BYU bishop, after the block of meetings each Sunday, my counselors and I took the time to go over the names of all the members who had not attended that day so I could determine if there was a problem I needed to address. One time I asked where a certain young man had been that day. My student executive secretary said, "He stayed up until 5:00 AM playing video games and was too tired to come to church today." I was shocked. This young man had been a full-time missionary less than three months previously. Now, his lack of video game–related discipline (temperance) meant he was at home asleep rather than worshipping the Lord on the Sabbath. I wish I could say this was an isolated occurrence.

Whether it's road rage, pornography, illegal drugs, overeating, or time-wasting, suffice it to say, temperance could not be more important in our twenty-first century world.

Political Temperance

The word *moderate* is often used in defining temperance. It is not necessary to be a so-called political moderate in order to be temperate. One may be conservative, liberal, or moderate, politically; however, in my view, we should avoid extreme political views. There are fringes on the political left and right that are definitely intemperate and seem to me to be hate-filled. I think a temperate Latter-day Saint in the United States can easily find a reasonable set of political beliefs within the mainstream positions of the Democratic and Republican parties. I also believe one aspect of being temperate is that we ought to be able to have respectful political discussions, even with those who disagree with us.

Temperance Includes Balance

Hammering away constantly on one gospel point does not show temperance. Temperance includes balance. We should not pick out favorite doctrines and emphasize them out of proportion with other important gospel doctrines. In his wonderful book *Teach Ye Diligently*, Boyd K. Packer likened the doctrines of the fulness of the gospel to a piano keyboard, "Some members of the Church who should know better pick out a hobby key or two and tap them incessantly, to the irritation of those around them. They can dull their own spiritual sensitivities. They lose track that there is a fulness of the gospel, and they become as individuals, like many churches have become. They may reject the fulness in preference to a favorite note. This becomes exaggerated and distorted, leading them away into apostasy."[5]

God Is Slow to Anger

One thing is certain: "The Lord is gracious, and full of compassion; slow to anger, and of great mercy. The Lord is good to all: and his tender mercies are over all his works" (Psalm 145:8–9; see also Nehemiah 9:17; Psalm 103:8; Joel 2:13; Jonah 4:2; Nahum 1:3). If we are to be like Him, we need to develop temperance, self-control, self-discipline, self-restraint, and moderation. We, too, must be slow to anger. We can do this. "He that is slow to anger is better than the mighty, and he that ruleth his spirit than he that taketh a city" (Proverbs 16:32).

The great publisher Horace Greeley said of my hero, Abraham Lincoln, "There was probably no year of [Lincoln's] life when he was not a wiser, cooler, and better man than he had been the year before."[6] In this context, being "cool" does not mean "with it" or "happening." It means that every year of his life Lincoln was a more temperate, disciplined man than he was the year before. What a great goal for all of us to work toward.

Taking Up Our Cross

We are to be "temperate in all things" (1 Corinthians 9:25; Alma 7:23; Alma 38:10; D&C 12:8). Or, as President George Q. Cannon said, "Temperance should govern in everything."[7] I like this beautiful addition to the New Testament from the Joseph Smith Translation:" Then said Jesus unto his disciples, If any man will come after me, let him deny himself, and take up his cross and follow me. *And now for a man to take up his cross, is to deny himself of all ungodliness, and every worldly lust, and keep my commandments*" (JST Matthew 16:25–26, emphasis added).

We take up our cross by denying ourselves of all ungodliness and every worldly lust. We can learn to exercise temperance by acting temperately. Aristotle taught that men acquire a particular quality by constantly acting a particular way: "It is by doing just acts that we become just, by doing temperate actions we become temperate, by doing courageous actions we become courageous."[8] Before we actually become a temperate person, we develop temperance, little by little, by practicing temperate acts. If we do enough temperate acts, eventually we become a temperate person.

Conclusion

I close this chapter on temperance with the words of President Spencer W. Kimball about temperance and the broader subject of taking upon ourselves the totality of the divine nature:

> Self-mastery, then, is the key, and every person should study his own life, his own desires and wants and cravings, and bring them under control. Man can transform himself and he must.
>
> Man has in himself the seeds of godhood, which can germinate and grow and develop. As the acorn becomes the oak, the mortal man becomes a god. It is within his power to lift himself by his very bootstraps from the plane on which he finds himself to the plane on which he should be. It may be a long, hard lift with many obstacles, but it is a real possibility.[9]

Summary

- To be temperate means to be moderate or self-restrained, not extreme in opinion or statement. Another word that sums up the concept of temperance is self-control.
- A temperate person is restrained in emotions and verbal expressions. He does not swear or take the Lord's name in vain.
- A bishop must be temperate and not soon angry.
- Temperance is one of the fruits of the Spirit. It means to be moderate and self-restrained in indulging appetites and passions.

- A temperate person can avoid many of the evils and problems of our time, such as unbridled anger, pornography, immorality, drug abuse, overeating, and time-wasting.
- We can be temperate in our political views, whether they are conservative or liberal.
- It is not temperate to plunk constantly on one gospel key.
- We are to be temperate in all things. When we "take up our cross" by denying ourselves of ungodliness and every worldly lust, we are being temperate.

Notes

1. Ezra Taft Benson, "Godly Characteristics of the Master," *Ensign*, Nov. 1986, 45, emphasis added.
2. Robert D. Hales, "Gifts of the Spirit," *Ensign*, Feb. 2002, 12.
3. David O. McKay, as quoted in Ezra Taft Benson, "What Manner of Men Ought We to Be," *Ensign*, Nov. 1983, 42.
4. Benson, "Godly Characteristics of the Master," 45.
5. Boyd K. Packer, *Teach Ye Diligently* (Salt Lake City: Deseret Book, 1975), 53–54.
6. Stefan Lorant, *The Life of Abraham Lincoln* (New York: The New American Library of World Literature, Inc., 1955), 218.
7. Cannon, *Gospel Truth*, vol. 2, 228.
8. Aristotle, *Nicomachean Ethics*, trans. J. E. C. Welldon (Amherst, New York: Prometheus Books, 1987), 43.
9. Spencer W. Kimball, "The Abundant Life," *Ensign*, July 1978, 3.

8

Diligence

Wherefore, now let every man learn his duty, and to act in the office in which he is appointed, in all diligence.

D&C 107:99

The John Johnson home in Hiram, Ohio, is a Church historical site. I have visited there several times with my family members, and it has become a sacred place to me. It is where Joseph and Emma Smith were staying when Joseph received Section 76 of the Doctrine and Covenants and when Joseph was tarred and feathered.

On the night of March 24, 1832, a dozen men burst into the John Johnson home. Joseph was exhausted, having stayed up late tending his adopted twins, who were ill. Now it was Emma's turn, and Joseph had just gone to bed. Joseph was pulled from his bed and dragged out of the house into the cold March night. The mobbers spoke of killing Joseph but settled upon stripping him of his clothing, pouring hot tar on his body, and then covering him with feathers. He was choked and scratched. They tried to pour a liquid, perhaps poison, down his throat, but Joseph clenched his teeth and would not budge. One of his teeth was chipped, and he spoke with a slight whistle in his "s" sounds thereafter.

When they had completed their evil deed, the mob scattered like the cockroaches they were. Joseph, whose ankle had been wrenched in the ordeal, hobbled back to the house. When Emma saw him, she mistook the tar for blood and fainted. Friends spent the rest of the evening scraping away the tar, picking off the feathers, and putting ointment on Joseph's burned and scratched body.

Joseph knew the identity of his attackers but amazingly he did not seek retribution. He could have commanded his loyal followers to "go get 'em," but he did not. He bore the persecution without returning violence for violence. Sadly, a few days later, one of his twins died from exposure to the elements, brought about by the events of that evening.

I quote now from Joseph's journal entry about this difficult trial: "By morning I was ready to be clothed again. This being the Sabbath morning, the people assembled for meeting at the usual hour of worship, and among them came also the mobbers. . . . With my flesh all scarified and defaced, I preached to the congregation as usual, and in the afternoon of the same day baptized three individuals."[1]

I leave for another time a discussion of the remarkable restraint Joseph showed in not seeking revenge. Joseph was a disciple of Jesus Christ—and he bore the persecution with magnificent patience and long-suffering. His forbearance on this occasion was indeed Christlike.

This chapter is about diligence. After the all-night travails, how about a Sabbath Day off for Joseph? No, there was no time off for the Lord's Prophet. There was a sermon to be preached, and there were three people to be baptized, so the Prophet went right back to work. He did his duty. In a word, he was diligent. Even before the events of that tragic evening, the Lord said of Joseph Smith: "Him have I inspired to move the cause of Zion in mighty power for good, *and his diligence I know*, and his prayers I have heard" (D&C 21:7, emphasis added).

I have served in bishoprics and branch presidencies most of my adult life. Most Sundays, I have arisen by 5:00 or 5:30 AM to carry out my Church responsibilities. I don't mind saying that some days it was hard to get up. Some days I didn't feel very well. Some Saturday nights I had to stay up late. But I always got up Sunday morning, and do you know why? Because I had an image burned into my mind and soul of the great Prophet, torn from his bed in the middle of the night, beaten and brutalized, tarred and feathered, picking the tar from his scarified skin—and the next day "preaching to the congregation and baptizing three individuals." I may have had a few late Saturday nights, and I may not have always felt well on Sunday morning, but I was never tarred and feathered in the middle of the night. The Prophet Joseph's example of diligence will ever live in my mind and heart.

Encouraged to Be Diligent

In introducing the Godlike virtues of the divine nature, the Apostle Peter starts by saying "giving all diligence" (2 Peter 1:5). I have found at least sixty-four scriptures that encourage us to be diligent. I think God is serious about our being diligent. A true disciple of Jesus Christ is diligent.

The following scriptures teach that we are to be diligent in keeping the commandments of God. For "Thou hast commanded us to keep thy precepts diligently (Psalm 119:4). And "Surely the Lord hath commanded us to do this thing; and shall we not be diligent in keeping the commandments of the Lord? (1 Nephi 4:34)

"And moreover, I shall give this people a name, that thereby they may be distinguished above all the people which the Lord God hath brought out of the land of Jerusalem; and this I do because they have been a diligent people in keeping the commandments of the Lord (Mosiah 1:11). Later in the Book of Mormon we read, "And now I would that ye should be humble, and be submissive and gentle; easy to be entreated; full of patience and long-suffering; being temperate in all things; *being diligent in keeping the commandments of God at all times*; asking for whatsoever things ye stand in need, both spiritual and temporal; always returning thanks unto God for whatsoever things ye do receive" (Alma 7:23, emphasis added).

In our day we have been given a specific promise: "Be faithful and diligent in keeping the commandments of God, and I will encircle thee in the arms of my love" (D&C 6:20; see also Joshua 22:5; Mosiah 4:6; D&C 18:8; 30:8; 1 Nephi 15:11; Enos 1:10; and Alma 39:1).

The Lord's Diligence

With diligence being a Christlike virtue, let us examine two or three examples of Christ's diligence. In my study of the life of the Savior, I don't recall Jesus ever turning someone away. He never seemed to have been in a hurry. He seemed always to have time for everyone.

His disciples apparently thought He was busy, but He said, "Suffer the little children to come unto me, and forbid them not: for of such is the kingdom of God" (Mark 10:14). After He learned of the death of John the Baptist, "he departed then by ship into a desert place apart" (Matthew 14:13). I think He was sad, and I think He wanted to be alone for a while. But when the people heard He was there, they followed Him, "and Jesus went forth, and saw a great multitude, and was moved with compassion toward them, and he healed their sick" (Matthew 14:14). He even worked a miracle so they would not go away hungry, feeding the five thousand (Matthew 14:15–21). In a word, He was diligent, even while mourning the loss of his friend, cousin, and fellow prophet.

In the New World, the resurrected Lord, though no longer burdened with physical fatigue, was still diligent in His service to the people. He allowed each person to come forth and touch Him. I wonder how long it took Him to give 2,500 people this individualized witness. In 3 Nephi 11 we read of this great act of love:

> Arise and come forth unto me, that ye may thrust your hands into my side, and also that ye may feel the prints of the nails in my hands and in my feet, that ye may know that I am the God of Israel, and the God of the whole earth, and have been slain for the sins of the world. And it came to pass that the multitude went forth, and thrust their hands into his side, and did feel the prints of the nails in his hands and in his feet; and this they did do, *going forth one by one until they had all gone forth*, and did see with their eyes and did feel with their hands, and did know of a surety and did bear record, that it was he, of whom it was written by the prophets, that should come. (3 Nephi 11:14–15, emphasis added)

When He discerned their reluctance to have him leave, he tarried longer, healing all their sick and blessing all their little children (see 3 Nephi 17).

The Savior's parable of the talents (see Matthew 25:14–30) is a masterful lesson in diligence. The servant who worked to turn five talents to ten and the servant who turned two talents to four were each praised as a "good and faithful servant" who had been "faithful over a few things" and thus would be made "ruler over many things." On the other hand, the servant who buried his talent was called a "wicked and slothful servant."

Not Running Faster than We Have Strength

Although the Lord requires diligence, He does not require us to do more than reasonably can be done. There must be balance. The Lord Himself did not run about hectically.

"And see that all these things are done in wisdom and order; for it is not requisite that a man should run faster than he has strength. And again, it is expedient that he should be diligent, that thereby he might win the prize; therefore, all things must be done in order" (Mosiah 4:27). In the Doctrine and Covenants, we are taught, "Do not run faster or labor more than you have strength and means . . . but be diligent unto the end" (D&C 10:4).

When my wife and I arrived in Korea, I heard the story of one of our great missionaries, Elder Jared Peterson. Prior to my arrival, Elder Peterson had worked on each preparation day. This bothered some of his companions, who complained to President Waddell, the previous mission president. President Waddell asked Elder Peterson why he worked on preparation day. Elder Peterson responded, "President, you told me to have fun on preparation day, and what could be more fun than teaching the gospel of Jesus Christ?" Despite Elder Peterson's great attitude and legendary diligence, President Waddell told him that he needed to rest and prepare on preparation day. Neither Elder Peterson nor his companions were to "run faster or labor more than they had strength."

Diligence in Gaining Knowledge

If we want to gain knowledge, we must seek it diligently. Diligence is linked to gaining knowledge—and knowledge itself is one of the Godlike virtues discussed in the following two scriptures.

From Alma, "It is given unto many to know the mysteries of God; nevertheless they are laid under a strict command that they shall not impart only according to the portion of his word which he doth grant unto the children of men, according to the heed and diligence which they give unto him" (Alma 12:9). "And if a person gains more knowledge and intelligence in this life through his diligence and obedience than another, he will have so much the advantage in the world to come" (D&C 130:19).

Blessings of Diligence

We know that "all victory and glory is brought to pass . . . through [our] diligence, faithfulness, and prayers of faith" (D&C 103:36). God is a "rewarder of them that diligently seek him" (Hebrews 11:6). As we are diligent, we "may be found of him in peace, without spot, and blameless" (2 Peter 3:14). As we are faithful and diligent, we will be "crowned with blessings from above," "with commandments not a few," and "with revelations in their time" (D&C 59:4). If we seek the Lord diligently, we will find Him (see D&C 88:63). If we "seek diligently the kingdom of heaven and its righteousness . . . all things necessary shall be added thereunto" (D&C 106:3).

In the Book of Mormon, the Liahona led the people "according to the heed and diligence they gave unto the [Lord]" (Mosiah 1:16). The Liahona can be likened to the Holy Ghost, "which is the gift of God unto all those who diligently seek him" (1 Nephi 10:17). The word of God is imparted unto the children of men according to the heed and diligence they give unto Him (see Alma 12:9). Peace and prosperity also come because of diligence and heeding the word of God (see Alma 49:30). Searching the scriptures diligently helps us know the word of God and profit thereby (see Alma 17:2; Mosiah 1:7).

Missionary Diligence

As full-time missionaries, each time we recited Section 4 of the Doctrine and Covenants, we listed "diligence" as one of the missionary qualifications. Missionaries are to be diligent even when the results of their labors are meager. That was what Mormon taught his beloved son Moroni when they were having a very hard time finding anyone willing to listen to them. "And now, my beloved son, notwithstanding their hardness, let us labor diligently; for if we should cease to labor, we should be brought under condemnation; for we have a labor to perform whilst in this tabernacle of clay, that we may conquer the enemy of all righteousness, and rest our souls in the kingdom of God" (Moroni 9:6).

Early in this dispensation, in September of 1839, two great missionaries, Brigham Young and Heber C. Kimball, set a stirring and heroic example of diligence and faithfulness as they left their families to serve a mission in England. Both men were sick, as were almost all of their family members. They only had one set of clothes because the mob in Missouri had taken nearly all their possessions. Of his farewell, Heber C. Kimball wrote:

> I went to my bed and shook hands with my wife, who was then shaking with the ague, and had two of our children lying sick by her side. I embraced her and my children, and bade them farewell. The only child well was little Heber Parley, and it was with difficulty that he could carry a couple of quarts of water at a time, to assist in quenching their thirst.
>
> With some difficulty we got into the wagon and started down the hill about ten rods. It seemed to me as though my very inmost parts would melt within me at the thought of leaving my family in such a condition, as it were almost in the arms of death. I felt as though I could scarcely endure it. I said to the teamster "hold up!" then turning to Brother Brigham I added, "This is pretty tough, but let's rise, and give them a cheer." We arose, and swinging our hats three times over our heads, we cried, "Hurrah, hurrah, hurrah for Israel!"
>
> My wife, hearing the noise, arose from her bed and came to the door to see what was up. She had a smile on her face. She and Sister Young then cried out to us, "Good bye; God bless you!" We returned the compliment and were pleased to see that they were so cheerful. We then told the driver to go ahead.
>
> After this I felt a spirit of joy and gratitude at having the satisfaction of seeing my wife standing upon her feet, instead of leaving her in bed, knowing well that I should not see her again for two or three years.[2]

Unwearyingness

Another great example of diligence is Nephi, the son of Helaman, in the Book of Mormon. The entire story to which I am referring is found in Helaman 10:1–19. Suffice it to say, Nephi had been tireless in his service to God. He had suffered greatly at the hands of the people. He had prophesied of the murder of the chief judge and had revealed the murderer's identity to the people. He had been misjudged and accused of complicity. When things were finally straightened out, and he was returning to his home, exhausted no doubt, this is what happened:

> And it came to pass that Nephi went his way towards his own

> house, pondering upon the things which the Lord had shown unto him.
>
> And it came to pass as he was thus pondering—being much cast down because of the wickedness of the people of the Nephites, their secret works of darkness, and their murderings, and their plunderings, and all manner of iniquities—and it came to pass as he was thus pondering in his heart, behold, a voice came unto him saying:
>
> Blessed art thou, Nephi, for those things which thou hast done; for I have beheld how thou hast with unwearyingness declared the word, which I have given unto thee, unto this people. And thou hast not feared them, and hast not sought thine own life, but hast sought my will, and to keep my commandments.
>
> And now, because thou hast done this with such unwearyingness, behold, I will bless thee forever; and I will make thee mighty in word and in deed, in faith and in works; yea, even that all things shall be done unto thee according to thy word, for thou shalt not ask that which is contrary to my will. (Helaman 10:2–5)

Isn't that a wonderful word—*unwearyingness*? Nephi was given power over the elements and power that whatever he said would be done. He was then commanded to return to the people and to command them to repent. I really like Nephi's response.

> And now behold, I command you, that ye shall go and declare unto this people, that thus saith the Lord God, who is the Almighty: Except ye repent ye shall be smitten, even unto destruction. And behold, now it came to pass that when the Lord had spoken these words unto Nephi, *he did stop and did not go unto his own house, but did return unto the multitudes who were scattered about upon the face of the land, and began to declare unto them the word of the Lord which had been spoken unto him, concerning their destruction if they did not repent.* (Helaman 10:11–12, emphasis added)

Persecuted, rejected, misjudged, and fatigued, Nephi "did stop and did not go unto his own house," but he went right back out and did the Lord's work. No wonder God loved him. No wonder God trusted him. *Unwearyingness* is not a word that appears in the dictionary, but what a great word it is. I hope someday God can say I did His work with unwearyingness.

Returning Speedily

Alma the Younger is also a great example to us. He was the former chief judge of the country. In our terminology, he was their former president. But he was rejected and ill-treated as he attempted to teach the gospel in the city of Ammonihah (see Alma 8:13–18). The people withstood all his words, reviled him, spat upon him, and cast him out of their city (see v. 13). As he was journeying away from Ammonihah, he was very sad because of the wickedness of the people. But, an angel appeared to him and said:

> Blessed art thou, Alma; therefore, lift up thy head and rejoice, for thou hast great cause to rejoice; for thou hast been faithful in keeping the commandments of God from the time which thou receivedst thy first message from him. Behold, I am he that delivered it unto you.
>
> And behold, I am sent to command thee that thou return to the city of Ammonihah, and preach again unto the people of the city; yea, preach unto them. Yea, say unto them, except they repent the Lord God will destroy them. . . .
>
> Now it came to pass that after Alma had received his message from the angel of the Lord he returned speedily to the land of Ammonihah. (Alma 8:15–16, 18)

Alma "returned speedily" to the place where he had so recently been reviled, spat upon, and cast out. He returned speedily to the place where his physical life was in danger. I love the diligence, faithfulness, obedience, and courage of Alma.

President Kimball's Diligence

When he was called as an apostle, Spencer W. Kimball was devastated. He felt that he was unqualified for such a high and noble calling. He cried himself to sleep for thirty nights in a row. Finally, in an answer to many prayers, he had this feeling: "If God needs a worker, then I'm his man. I may not be the most gifted, but I can be the most diligent." And oh, was he diligent! He arose each morning at 5:00 and worked until midnight many days, taking cat-naps to get him through. His mantras were "Do it" (before the Nike company), "Lengthen your stride," and "Quicken your pace." He simply showed God his love and devotion by working harder than everyone else. I love and honor President Kimball for his diligence. And, by the way, he *was* gifted as well as diligent.

Diligence in Non-Spiritual Matters

The principle of diligence also applies to non-spiritual matters, such as work and education. This was my weekly schedule when I attended law school from 1977 to 1980:

Weekdays

5:00 AM Arise; read scriptures; shower; eat breakfast
6:00 AM Arrive at law library to begin studying
(Study and attend classes)
5:00 PM Go jogging
(Have dinner with Janet)
7:00 PM Back to the law library to study
10:00 PM Home from the law library; go to bed

Saturday

5:00 AM Arise; read scriptures; shower; eat breakfast
6:00 AM Arrive at law library to begin studying
2:00 PM Go home; have a family activity with Janet and our daughter, Laura Anne

Sunday

No studying; attend church; fulfill calling as a first counselor in a married student ward bishopric; enjoy family time

It was very hard to live this schedule. At the time, many of my friends were enjoying life. Some of them never attended college. Others attended college but not graduate school. Keeping this schedule required diligence on my part. But it was an investment, and it was worth it. Because I lived this schedule, I was later able to have interesting jobs that provided me with a good living and allowed me to support my wife and children. Diligence applies to all aspects of our lives, not just our Church service.

Diligence in Church Callings

My parents-in-law, Richard and Cenia Parsons, have always set a great example of diligent service, both to their family and in their Church callings. I remember when they were ward nursery leaders.

They took their calling very seriously and served with great enthusiasm and creativity. I also served with them in the BYU Seventh Stake, and they served as our mission office couple when I was a mission president. In every calling, they have served with devotion and diligence.

My wife, Janet, must have learned from observing her parents in action, because she is the most diligent Church servant I know. Whatever her calling may be, she performs it with exceeding diligence and enthusiasm. She can't really understand anyone who is slothful or less than anxiously engaged. In her growing maturity, she is patient and long-suffering with others who are less committed, but she really can't understand not being completely faithful.

"I'd Do Anything for the Lord"

Is there anything too good for the Lord? Shouldn't we give Him our absolute best effort? Years ago, when I served as a young missionary, whenever we had to do something hard, my companion and I would look at each other and say, "Elder, I'd do anything for the Lord." When a Korean offered us a seafood item not indigenous to Utah, we'd look at each other and say, "I'd do anything for the Lord, Elder. How about you?" And then, even though we didn't know how we could possibly choke it down, we'd eat it.

On a cold winter morning, with only ice cold water for our shower, one of us would say, "I'll go first; I'd do anything for the Lord." The same response held true when it was raining or snowing and it was time to go proselyting: "Let's go, Elder. We'd do anything for the Lord." As young missionaries, we were greatly blessed for our diligence. No matter what we are called to do, it helps our performance if we consider that we are doing it for the Lord.

Diligence in Parenting

Nephi said, "We labor diligently to write, to persuade our children, and also our brethren, to believe in Christ, and to be reconciled to God" (2 Nephi 25:23). Speaking of children, parents—especially mothers—labor diligently to raise their young children. As I watch my daughters Laura and Mary with their young children, I am amazed at the time, energy, and patience it takes to be a loving mother of children. I marvel that my wife was able to do this so well for our six children.

As I sit on the stand in the chapel during sacrament meeting and watch the young mothers and fathers struggle with their little children, my heart is filled with gratitude for their diligence in bringing their little ones to church each Sunday. I know that God will bless them for their diligent service to their children, both in the home and at church.

We are to "be diligent in all things" (D&C 75:29). One night, when serving as a BYU bishop, I received an emergency call from a young woman in our ward. Her abusive stepfather had come into town unexpectedly and was looking for her. In the middle of the night, I secretly took her to the battered women's shelter in Provo for her protection. I had to sign a non-disclosure agreement, promising never to divulge the location of the shelter. After she was settled, I drove toward my home in Orem. It was about 3:30 in the morning, and I had to be at work by 8:00 AM. As I was driving, I had a warm feeling in my heart—a cleansing, sanctifying feeling. The following words were whispered into my mind: "I know what you have done, and I know I can count on you, day or night." I felt very good, despite the lack of sleep.

Conclusion

Diligence is a divine virtue. It is also a decision. Diligence is a gift we can give God in appreciation for His many blessings. "We'd do anything for the Lord!" I know that God is a rewarder of those who diligently seek and serve Him.

Summary

- The Prophet Joseph set a great example of diligence when he went right back to work after being tarred and feathered in Hiram, Ohio.
- At least sixty-four scriptures encourage us to be diligent. (Apparently, God is serious about it!)
- Jesus set an example of diligence in the way He responded to the people who desired His healing touch. He taught diligence through His parable of the talents.
- God requires diligence but does not ask us to do more than we reasonably can do. The Lord Himself did not rush around hectically.
- Diligence is linked to gaining knowledge. We are to give diligent

heed to the Lord. Full-time missionaries must serve diligently.

- Book of Mormon prophets like Alma the Younger and Nephi, the son of Helaman, showed dramatic examples of diligence in performing their ministries. Nephi served with "unwearyingness."
- President Spencer W. Kimball was an example of diligence in his ministry.
- Diligence is helpful in our worldly studies.
- We should perform our Church callings with diligence.
- Diligence is a gift we can give to God for His many blessings given so graciously to us. "We'd do anything for the Lord."

Notes

1. Joseph Smith, *History of The Church of Jesus Christ of Latter-day Saints*, vol 1, 264.
2. Stanley B. Kimball, "Heber C. Kimball and Family, The Nauvoo Years," BYU Studies, vol. 15 (1974–75), no. 4 (Summer 1975), 449

9

Kindness and Gentleness

My dear children, I am very anxious that you should know something about the History of Jesus Christ. For everybody ought to know about Him. No one ever lived, who was so good, so kind, so gentle, and so sorry for all people who did wrong, or were in any way ill or miserable, as he was.

—*Charles Dickens*[1]

George Albert Smith, eighth president of the Church, was known for his kind and loving nature. One day while his car was parked in downtown Salt Lake City, a blanket was stolen from it. That night he wrote in his journal: "If I thought the man who took it really needed it I would have presented it to him and he would not have been a thief."[2] He was not angry that he had lost his blanket; instead, he felt bad that the man who took it had become a thief.

When President Smith died, his successor, President David O. McKay, said he "lived as nearly as it is humanly possible for a man to live a Christlike life."[3] What a tribute! President Smith's life is evidence that with God's refining influence and with our own patient effort, we can make significant progress during this life on our pathway to perfection.

THE FATHER AND SON ARE KIND AND GENTLE

This chapter is about the Godlike attributes of kindness and gentleness. The Father and Son are kind and gentle. In describing Them, the scriptures use the words "loving kindness," "everlasting kindness, and "great kindness" (Nehemiah 9:17; Psalm 51:1; Isaiah 54:8; Isaiah 63:7; D&C 133:52). God is even "kind unto the unthankful and to the evil" (Luke 6:35). In listing some of the Christlike virtues, the Apostle Peter included "brotherly kindness" (2 Peter 1:7). Disciples of Christ are kind and gentle, tender and mild, considerate and benevolent, amiable and sympathetic, gracious and humane. They are not coarse, rough, brusque, vindictive, or unfeeling. People are important, and a follower of Christ is sensitive to the feelings of others.

Although Jesus was bold in confronting sin and evil, He was kind and gentle to the many people who crossed his path. He was quick to forgive the repentant sinner, including the woman caught in adultery, to whom He said, "Neither do I condemn thee: go, and sin no more" (John 8:11). His kindness was exemplified by His many acts of healing. He was never too busy to minister unto the people. I like the chorus from the children's song "I'm Trying to Be Like Jesus," by Janice Kapp Perry:

> Love one another as Jesus loves you.
> Try to show kindness in all that you do.
> Be gentle and loving in deed and in thought,
> For these are the things Jesus taught.[4]

These are not only the things Jesus taught; these are the things Jesus did.

The Atonement is a manifestation of Jesus' loving kindness. We read in the Book of Mormon: "And the world, because of their iniquity, shall judge him to be a thing of naught; wherefore they scourge him, and he suffereth it; and they smite him, and he suffereth it. Yea, they spit upon him, and he suffereth it, *because of his loving kindness* and his long-suffering towards the children of men" (1 Nephi 19:9, emphasis added).

Gentleness, mercy, and forgiveness are the essence of Christianity, as Charles Dickens explained to his children:

> Remember!—It is christianity TO DO GOOD always—even

to those who do evil to us. It is christianity to love our neighbour as ourself, and to do to all men as we would have them Do to us. It is christianity to be gentle, merciful, and forgiving, and to keep those qualities quiet in our own hearts, and never make a boast of them, or of our prayers or of our love of God, but always to shew that we love Him by humbly trying to do right in everything. If we do this, and remember the life and lessons of Our Lord Jesus Christ, and try to act up to them, we may confidently hope that God will forgive us our sins and mistakes, and enable us to live and die in Peace.[5]

Kindness of Mere Mortals

We have many examples of kindness and gentleness in the lives of our prophets and other leaders and friends. As you know by now, Lincoln is one of my personal heroes. A contemporary journalist wrote that Lincoln was "too kind for bitterness and too great for vituperation."[6] When Lincoln needed to write a letter taking corrective action or relieving a general or other leader from his post, he wrote a first draft in which he said exactly what he thought. Those first drafts were filled with anger and sarcasm. Then, Lincoln would put the letter aside and wait a day or two. At that point, he would write a second, kinder letter and send that one. He still took the needed action (such as firing a military general), but he did it with as much kindness and tact as possible under the circumstances.[7]

John M. Bernhisel, a man who boarded with the Smith family for more than nine months, shared these impressions of Joseph Smith to Illinois Governor Ford in 1844:

> General Joseph Smith is naturally a man of strong mental powers, and is possessed of much energy and decision of character, great penetration, and a profound knowledge of human nature. He is a man of calm judgment, enlarged views, and is eminently distinguished by his love of justice. *He is kind and obliging, generous and benevolent, sociable and cheerful*, and is possessed of a mind of a contemplative and reactive character. He is honest, frank, fearless and independent, and as free from dissimulation as any man to be found.
>
> But it is in the gentle charities of domestic life, as the *tender and affectionate husband and parent, the warm and sympathizing friend*, that the prominent traits of his character are revealed, and his heart

is felt to be keenly alive to the *kindest and softest emotions* of which human nature is susceptible.[8]

I think how a man treats little children is a good indicator of his character. This is a recollection from a young child who had an interaction with the Prophet Joseph:

> My older brother and I were going to school, near to the building which was known as Joseph's brick store. It had been raining the previous day, causing the ground to be very muddy, especially along that street. My brother Wallace and I both got [our feet] in the mud, and could not get out, and of course, child-like, we began to cry, for we thought we would have to stay there. But looking up, I beheld the loving friend of children, the Prophet Joseph, coming to us. He soon had us on higher and drier ground. Then he stooped down and cleaned the mud from our little, heavy-laden shoes, took his handkerchief from his pocket and wiped our tear-stained faces. He spoke kind and cheering words to us, and sent us on our way to school rejoicing.[9]

President Harold B. Lee is a good example of a man who developed a gentle nature as he went through life, showing that we can overcome our natural tendencies. From the *Encyclopedia of Mormonism* we learn, "President Lee's spirituality resulted partly from his personal struggles. He learned to control a fiery temper and a quick, action-oriented disposition that had earlier in his life offended some. In his later years, President Lee was perceived as being more gentle in manner, compassionate, gracious, hospitable, and thoughtful of others."[10]

Persons who interacted with our fifth Church president, Lorenzo Snow, commented on his gentle nature:

> Lorenzo Snow was small and slender in appearance. He stood five feet, six inches tall, weighed 140 pounds, and had tranquil gray eyes and a full beard. He was a scholar, schoolmaster, missionary, legislator, cooperative leader, financier, temple worker, and prophet. He had a profound effect upon Latter-day Saints and non-Mormons alike, with his heavenly countenance and sweet, gentle dignity. Meeting him for the first time, a Protestant minister said, "I was startled to see the holiest face I had ever been privileged to look upon. . . . The strangest feeling stole over me, that I stood on holy ground." Another minister said, "The tenor of his spirit is as gentle

> as a child. You are introduced to him. You are pleased with him. You converse with him, you like him. You visit with him long . . . , you love him."[11]

The "fruit of the Spirit is love, joy, peace, longsuffering, gentleness, goodness, faith" (Galatians 5:22). And "the wisdom that is from above is first pure, then peaceable, gentle, and easy to be intreated, full of mercy and good fruits, without partiality, and without hypocrisy" (James 3:17). The "servant of the Lord must not strive; but be gentle unto all men, apt to teach, patient" (2 Timothy 2:24). And saints are to "speak evil of no man, to be no brawlers, but gentle, shewing all meekness unto all men" (Titus 3:2).

The Apostle Paul said, "Let the husband render unto the wife due benevolence: and likewise also the wife unto the husband" (1 Corinthians 7:3). We believe in being benevolent (Articles of Faith 1:13). Benevolence means kindness and good will. With half the marriages in the United States ending in divorce, benevolence between husband and wife would be a most welcome thing.

I have had three young men ask for my three daughters' hands in marriage. Each time, as I gave my blessing, I told my future son-in-law that I expected him to treat my daughter with the utmost kindness. I told him if he ever laid a hand on my daughter in anger, he and I were going to have a major problem. I told him that if he was unfaithful to my daughter, breaking her tender heart, he and I would have a major problem. So far, my sons-in-law have kept their promise to me.

Strangely, I have found that people tend to be kinder to total strangers than they are to the people closest to them. I often see married people and parents and children saying rude things to each other and being unkind in public. I think we should be especially kind to the people who are closest to us—and no one is closer than our husband or wife.

Priesthood leaders (and, in my view, parents) are subject to this wise principle from the Doctrine and Covenants: "No power or influence can or ought to be maintained by virtue of the priesthood, only by persuasion, by long-suffering, by gentleness and meekness, and by love unfeigned" (D&C 121:41).

I hesitate to use myself as a good example, but please recall that I used my anger management problem as a bad example in a previous chapter. I have tried to be kind and gentle as a father. I recall vividly times as a father when I could have been kinder and gentler. But I was gratified and felt I had succeeded at least to some extent, when just recently my wife wrote a blog post about a sharing time that our daughter Laura had given as the Primary president in her ward in upstate New York. My wife wrote,

> Laura told us Sunday about how she used an experience from her childhood to teach her Primary children about how fathers preside over their families.
>
> In 1987, when we lived in a rented apartment in Seoul, Korea, [our daughters] Laura and Mary shared a room and a full-sized bed that was provided by the owner of the apartment. They occasionally jumped on the bed, even though they knew they weren't supposed to. One evening, an older (and larger) friend was visiting; she joined the girls in jumping on the bed, and it broke. The girls were scared, but knew they had to confess, so they told Rich the bed was broken. He reminded them they weren't supposed to be jumping on the bed, especially since we didn't even own it, but he concluded by showing forth an increase of love and telling them that "people are more important than things."
>
> This theme carried through during the kids' driving years; whenever they scratched or dented a car, he would always ask if they were okay and remind them that "people are more important than things."
>
> Last night, after dinner, [our youngest son] Michael, Rich, and I were relaxing and visiting on the new Ikea corner sofa; Michael was a little frustrated by all the pillows on the sofa and said, "Why do we have to have so many pillows on this couch?" Rich replied, "Because Mom likes them, and we like her."
>
> My heart was touched by Rich's comment. I know he doesn't like all the pillows on the sofas or on our bed, but he never complains because he knows they make me happy.
>
> Thanks to my dear husband for teaching our children and reminding me that "people are more important than things.[12]

It is easier to be kind and gentle with people when we remember that people are more important than things. People are what God is all about. His work and glory is "to bring to pass the immortality and eternal life of man" (Moses 1:39).

Conclusion

Kindness is part of charity, for "charity suffereth long and is kind" (1 Corinthians 13:4). Paul also taught: "And be ye kind one to another, tenderhearted, forgiving one another, even as God for Christ's sake hath forgiven you" (Ephesians 4:32). We close this chapter with the teachings of President Howard W. Hunter, who echoed the thoughts of the Apostle Paul.

> The world in which we live . . . needs the gospel of Jesus Christ. It provides the only way the world will ever know peace. We need to be kinder with one another, more gentle and forgiving. We need to be slower to anger and more prompt to help. We need to extend the hand of friendship and resist the hand of retribution. In short, we need to love one another with the pure love of Christ, with genuine charity and compassion and, if necessary, shared suffering, for that is the way God loves us.[13]

Summary

- It is possible for a human to live a very Christlike life. President George Albert Smith was a good example in that regard.
- God and Jesus are kind and gentle. The scriptures use such words as "loving kindness," "everlasting kindness," and "great kindness."
- Jesus was bold in confronting sin and evil, but He was kind to the many people who crossed His path. He was quick to forgive the repentant sinner. The Atonement is the supreme manifestation of the Lord's loving kindness.
- Disciples of Christ are kind and gentle, tender and mild, considerate and benevolent, amiable and sympathetic, gracious and humane. They are not coarse, rough, brusque, vindictive, or unfeeling.
- Abraham Lincoln was known for his kindness, as was the Prophet Joseph Smith. President Lorenzo Snow was sweet and gentle. President Harold B. Lee learned to control a fiery temper and an action-oriented disposition, and in his later years was perceived as being gentle in manner, compassionate, gracious, hospitable, and thoughtful of others.
- Gentleness is a fruit of the Spirit. A servant of God must be gentle. Husbands and wives should be kind and gentle with each other. Parents also need to be kind and gentle with their children.

- It helps to be kind and gentle if we remember that people are more important than things.
- Kindness is a manifestation of charity, the pure love of Christ.

Notes

1. Charles Dickens, *The Life of Our Lord* (London: Associated Newspapers, 1934; reprinted Philadelphia: Westminster Press), 11.
2. Preston Nibley, *The Presidents of the Church* (Salt Lake City: Deseret Book, 1974), 285–86.
3. "George Albert Smith 'Never Departed' from Gospel Goals," LDS Church News, Nov. 11, 1989.
4. *Children's Songbook* (Salt Lake City: The Church of Jesus Christ of Latter-Day Saints, 1989), 78.
5. Dickens, *The Life of Our Lord*, 124–27.
6. Albert D. Richardson, "Field Dungeon and Escape," in *Intimate Memories of Lincoln*, ed. Rufus Rockwell Wilson (Elmira, NY: Primavera Press, 1945), 212–13.
7. See Douglas Wilson, *Lincoln's Sword*, 199.
8. Joseph Smith, *History of The Church of Jesus Christ of Latter-day Saints*, vol. 6, 468, emphasis added.
9. Margaret McIntire Burgess, as quoted in Leon R. Hartshorn, *Classic Stories from the Lives of Our Prophets* (Salt Lake City: Deseret Book, 1971), 13.
10. *Encyclopedia of Mormonism*, 823.
11. Ibid., 1370.
12. Janet Rife, http://jprserenity.blogspot.com/search?updated-max=2009-03-16T11%3A33%3A00-06%3A00&max-results=7
13. Howard W. Hunter, "A More Excellent Way," *Ensign*, May 1992, 61.

10

Easiness in Being Entreated

Elder Oaks of the Quorum of the Twelve concluded that through his extensive personal research, the Joseph [Smith] he came to meet was a man of the frontier: young, emotional, dynamic, and so loved and approachable by his people that they often called him "Brother Joseph."

—*LDS Church News*[1]

MANY YEARS AGO, WHEN I was a young man, I had a dear friend who made a serious mistake with his girlfriend. He made an appointment with his bishop, a stern man, and frankly confessed his sin. The bishop was very upset and told him rather harshly that he would likely suffer serious Church discipline.

After the appointment, my friend did not feel understood, comforted, or relieved in any way about the situation, so without an appointment he stopped by the home our of our stake president, William J. Pratt. President Pratt was a diminutive man, standing only five feet six inches tall, but his spirit was large. He had the image of God in his countenance.

President Pratt warmly invited my friend into his den. My friend began confess his sin. As he did so, he cried. His head was down as he told his sad tale. When he looked up to meet President Pratt's eyes, he noticed that tears were streaming down President Pratt's face. He was "mourn[ing] with those that [mourned]" (see Mosiah 18:9). President Pratt arose, walked around the desk, took my friend in his arms, and called him by name. "I'm so sorry," said President Pratt. "This will be difficult, but I will help you every step of the way, and we will get through this together, with the help of the Lord and His Atonement."

President Pratt did help him every step of the way. My friend and his girlfriend (who is now his wife) have lived an exemplary LDS life and have raised their many children in the gospel.

Bill Pratt was a gifted Church leader. He was handsome, with wavy black hair when he was young and wavy white hair when he was older. He had charisma and enthusiasm. He beamed all over. When he laughed, he laughed loudly, and his entire body shook with mirth. When someone said something sad or touching, he wept openly, wiping the tears that flowed freely down his face. He had a beautiful tenor voice, and when he sang, he sang at the top of his lungs. President Pratt warmly greeted everyone who came to church—and when he greeted you, you had his rapt attention. He was beloved by his ward and stake members. President Pratt did not have the slightest hint of arrogance, nor did he have a judgmental bone in his body. He loved everyone—and everyone eventually loved him. He is one of two main reasons (my mother being the number one reason) that my father returned to the Church from inactivity.

Of all the many leadership gifts and personality traits of Bill Pratt, one was clearly his approachability; he was easy to be entreated.

Being Easily Entreated

Being easily entreated is one of the divine virtues (see Alma 7:23), but it is not often talked or written about. It means being approachable, easy to meet or talk to. It means being accessible, easy to deal with, open, and friendly. A person who is easy to be entreated is reasonable, willing to listen and to hear opposing views with respectfulness. Such a person is not unapproachable, inaccessible, stubborn, controlling, or overbearing.

Since a divine attribute is, by definition, a Godlike attribute, we would expect to find that God is easy to be entreated and approachable. And so He is. He wants us to approach Him through prayer. I have found at least sixty-four references in the scriptures where God has said, "Ask and ye shall receive" or "Ask and it shall be given you" or something similar. He clearly wants us to entreat Him. He would prefer, however, that we ask not amiss, as evidenced in the New Testament, "Ye ask, and receive not, because *ye ask amiss*, that ye may consume it upon your lusts" (James 4:3, emphasis added). And in the Book of Mormon, "Yea, I know that God will give liberally to him that asketh. Yea, my God will give me, *if I ask not amiss*; therefore I will lift up my voice unto thee; yea, I will cry unto thee, my God, the rock of my righteousness" (2 Nephi 4:35, emphasis added). Later in the Book of Mormon, we also find this evidence, "And whatsoever ye shall ask the Father in my name, *which is right*, believing that ye shall receive, behold it shall be given unto you" (3 Nephi 18:20, emphasis added).

Young Joseph Entreated God

The scripture that launched this last dispensation was about entreating God. Young Joseph read, "If any of you lack wisdom, let him ask of God, that giveth to all men liberally, and upbraideth not; and it shall be given him" (James 1:5). And then Joseph walked into the grove and asked the question that was on his mind. My dear friend Heather Clark loves the words "upbraideth not" in this scripture. She says, "it is God's way of saying there are no dumb questions."

James taught how to recognize God's wisdom: "But the wisdom that is from above is first pure, then peaceable, gentle, and *easy to be intreated*, full of mercy and good fruits, without partiality, and without hypocrisy" (James 3:17, emphasis added).

Jesus Was Approachable

Jesus was approachable and easily entreated. The New Testament is full of examples of humble souls approaching Jesus and entreating Him to exercise His healing power on their behalf. He did not disappoint them, provided they had faith to be healed. In the Book of Mormon, 2,500 people were allowed to approach Jesus and thrust their hands into His side and feel the prints of the nails in His hands and feet so that they would know He was the God of the whole earth and had been slain for the sins of the world (see 3 Nephi 11:14–15). That is being approachable—literally. In 3 Nephi 17, Jesus perceived that the people did not want Him to leave, so He stayed with them longer, healing their sick and blessing their little children.

Perhaps the most memorable example of Jesus' approachability is His reaction when He learned that His disciples had turned away some children. "But when Jesus saw it, he was much displeased, and said unto them, Suffer the little children to come unto me, and forbid them not: for of such is the kingdom of God" (Mark 10:14; see also Matthew 19:14; Luke 18:16).

Elder Neal A. Maxwell said, "The man and woman of Christ are easily entreated, but the selfish person is not. Christ never brushed aside those in need because He had bigger things to do!"[2]

Examples of Approachability

Speaking of being a "man or woman of Christ," President Spencer W. Kimball was such a man. Elder Richard L. Evans said, "This is a rare man—Spencer Kimball—*as approachable as a child*, as wise as a father, as loving as a gentle brother."[3]

President James E. Faust said that President Howard W. Hunter was a man who was easy to be entreated.[4] I did not know President Hunter personally, but my friend Deanne Matheny did. Deanne and her husband, Ray, taught at the Jerusalem Center when then-Elder Hunter was deeply involved with that institution. Deanne told me that Elder Hunter was a kind and humble soul, who loved people and took an interest in them. He was easy to talk to. Whenever he met a new person, Elder Hunter would speak very little of himself, but with sincerity would ask the person all about himself or herself. His conversations were "others-focused." People who met Elder Hunter instinctively liked him; perhaps they did not realize that they liked him because he showed interest in them and let them talk about themselves.

I once received a compliment that was at once flattering and sad. My daughter Jenny told me of a friend who had made a mistake with her boyfriend and needed to repent of this transgression. Jenny reported that her friend had said to her, "If your dad were my bishop, I would confess my sin to him, but my bishop is too scary." I was disappointed to hear this because every member deserves to have a bishop who is easily entreated. Remember my friend from the beginning of this chapter? He was fortunate to have a stake president who was easily entreated—and that made a major difference in his life.

How to Become Easy to Entreat

If we are by nature friendly, outgoing, easygoing, and sociable, people may perceive us as being approachable and easy to be entreated. However, if we are by nature quiet, reserved, and shy, people may perceive us as unapproachable or hard to talk to. Is it possible to become approachable if this is not our natural strength or personality trait? Yes, it is. We had many missionaries in our mission who, prior to their missions, were not outgoing. They learned over time, and with some pain, to be friendlier and more outgoing, to strike up a conversation, and to talk with strangers.

It may not be easy, but it can be done. To be approachable, we have to be friendly. We must appear (and better yet, *be*) humble and self-effacing, not pompous or arrogant. We have to show an interest in people, like President Hunter did. We need to smile and look people in the eye. It may be hard, but we can do it. With practice, it becomes easier.

Another way to say this is that to be easily entreated we must be and appear "willing." If people know we are willing to serve, it is easier to ask us to serve. If you are the elders quorum president and you know that your fellow member Steven Whiteside is willing to help in any way possible, it is easy to entreat Steven when help is needed. As a parent, if you know one child helps cheerfully, while another always grumbles when asked, it is easier to entreat the non-grumbler (note: if the grumbler is a teenager, don't give up; he or she may grow out of it). "Behold, the Lord requireth the heart and a *willing* mind" (D&C 64:34, emphasis added). When we have a willing heart and mind, we are easily entreated.

Blessing of Being Easily Entreated

The blessing of being easy to be entreated is that we will, in fact, be entreated. This will give us an opportunity to serve. Even the Son of God came to earth to serve and not to be served. This is what He taught His disciples when He washed their feet, "Know ye what I have done to you? Ye call me Master and Lord: and ye say well; for so I am. If I then, your Lord and Master, have washed your feet; ye also ought to wash one another's feet. For I have given you an example, that ye should do as I have done to you. Verily, verily, I say unto you, The servant is not greater than his lord; neither he that is sent greater than he that sent him. If ye know these things, happy are ye if ye do them" (John 13:12–17). We will be happy as we follow the Savior's example and serve others.

Jesus is the great example of the servant-leader. After their improper request to sit on His right and left hand when He came in His glory, Jesus instructed James and John, "Ye know that they which are accounted to rule over the Gentiles exercise lordship over them; and their great ones exercise authority upon them. But so shall it not be among you: but whosoever will be great among you, shall be your minister: And whosoever of you will be the chiefest, shall be servant of all. For even the Son of man came not to be ministered unto, but to minister, and to give his life a ransom for many" (Mark 10:42–45). If we are to be His followers, if we are to be Christlike, we need to become servant-leaders, as He is.

When we moved into the mission home in Daejeon, Korea, my wife asked our assistant, Elder Timothy Glover, whom we had just met, to help her move some furniture. She indicated to Elder Glover that she knew it wasn't his job to move furniture and that she was sorry for asking. He cheerfully responded, "That's okay, Sister Rife, I'm happy to do it. I came here to serve." After that, my wife never hesitated to ask Elder Glover for his help, for she knew he had come to Korea to serve. It was easy to entreat him.

Not long ago, Janet was called to serve as Relief Society secretary. Our Relief Society president is Shari Sanders, a delightful, charming, hospitable sister who puts her whole heart and soul into her calling. I cannot imagine a better, more diligent Relief Society president anywhere in the Church. At first, it seemed that Sister Sanders hesitated to ask Janet to do things, not wanting to unduly infringe upon her time. However, after a little while, Sister Sanders realized that Janet is fully engaged in the work of the Lord—in other words, that Janet "came to serve." So now, Sister Sanders easily and frequently asks Janet for her help, knowing that Janet wants to be with her in the trenches, doing the work.

Conclusion

The children of God need to feel comfortable asking a servant-leader for help. They will only feel comfortable doing so if we are approachable, easily entreated, accessible, kindly, easy to deal with, open, friendly, and willing. It will be easy to entreat us if they know we "came to serve." We will be greatly blessed when we have the opportunity to serve Heavenly Father's other children.

Summary

- Being easy to be entreated is one of the Christlike virtues. It means to be approachable, easy to meet or talk to.
- A person who is easily entreated is accessible, easy to deal with, open, friendly, reasonable, willing to listen, and willing to hear opposing views with respectfulness. Such a person is not unapproachable, inaccessible, stubborn, controlling, or overbearing.
- The Father and Son are easily entreated. The statement "ask and ye shall receive," or something similar, is repeated at least sixty-four times in the scriptures.
- The New Testament is full of examples of humble souls entreating Jesus to exercise His healing power in their behalf. Jesus said, "Suffer the little children to come unto me."
- This last dispensation was launched when young Joseph entreated God as he had been instructed to do in James 1:5.
- One way to be easily entreated is to be others-focused in our conversations, like President Howard W. Hunter.
- People are more likely to approach us if we are friendly, outgoing, easygoing, sociable, and interested in people. Even if these are not our natural strengths, we can learn to act this way. We need to do this, especially if we hold a position such as bishop.
- Others will be more likely to entreat us if we are clearly willing to serve.
- It is a blessing to be entreated; it is a blessing to us to be able to serve others. We will be happy as we follow the Savior's example and serve others.

Notes

1. "Youthful Joseph Tempered Quickly in Furnace of Life," LDS Church News, April 13, 1996.
2. Neal A. Maxwell, "Put Off the Natural Man, and Come Off Conqueror," *Ensign*, Nov. 1990, 14.
3. Richard L. Evans, "President Kimball of the Council of the Twelve," *Improvement Era*, October 1954, emphasis added.
4. James E. Faust, "Howard W. Hunter: Man of God," *Ensign*, Apr. 1995, 26–28.

11

Holiness, Godliness, and Virtue

Righteousness is ultimately synonymous with holiness or godliness. . . . The terms "righteous" and "righteousness" also apply to mortals who, though beset with weaknesses and frailties, are seeking to come unto Christ. In this sense, righteousness is not synonymous with perfection. It is a condition in which a person is moving toward the Lord, yearning for godliness, continuously repenting of sins, and striving honestly to know and love God and to follow the principles and ordinances of the gospel.

—*Encyclopedia of Mormonism*[1]

Several years ago, our family moved into the mission home in Daejeon, Korea. That was pretty exciting for me as the mission president, but less exciting for my children who were nine, twelve, and fourteen years old at the time. You see, the children were the only English-speaking Latter-day Saint youth in Daejeon. And, while Daejeon is a good place to serve a mission, it's not that fun if you're an American child or teenager.

One day, early in our stay, Michael (age 9) was running around the living room of the mission home and jumping on the furniture. I had asked him before not to do this. Finally, in frustration, in my sternest voice, I said, "Michael, if you do that again I'm going to ground you." Jenny (age 12) immediately began to laugh. I asked, "Why are you laughing, Jenny?" She responded, "Dad, you can't ground Michael. The Church has already grounded all of us here in Daejeon for the next three years!"

Jenny was right—and we all had a good laugh. We had been grounded, but at least we were grounded in a holy place—for the mission home in Daejeon, Korea became for us a holy place. It was the site of new missionary orientation (We were in the *Orient*, so we had to have *orient*ation), the site of zone leader council, and the site of testimony meetings held the night before our valiant missionaries finished their missions and returned home. After our mission, Janet received a picture frame as a gift. The frame said, "Some moments we never forget because our lives have been forever changed by them." After much thought, Janet decided to put in that frame a picture of us with our elders following zone leader council at the mission home; it was a moment she never wanted to forget.

This chapter is on holiness, godliness, and virtue, three similar, interrelated attributes. Standing in holy places, such as temples, chapels, and our homes, is certainly one way to help develop these Christlike attributes in our lives. We should stand in holy places, but, as Michael learned, not necessarily on the furniture.

Holiness, Godliness, and Virtue

Holiness means being saintly, godly, pious, devout, and devoted to the service of God. Godliness means being religious, saintly, holy, and conforming to the laws and wishes of God. Virtue can be defined as moral excellence, goodness, purity, righteousness, chastity, integrity, and conformity of one's life to moral principles.

The word *holy* is used many times in the scriptures, most often as an adjective describing something else: Holy Ghost, holy angels, holy scriptures, holy writ, holy apostles, holy prophets, Holy Spirit, holy calling, holy priesthood, holy commandments, holy city, holy land, holy temple, and holy places. We know that the Father and Son are holy, for they are referred to as the Holy Father, the Holy One of Israel, and the Holy Messiah.

Holy Men and Women

There are also a number of men in the scriptures who are referred to as "holy men," such as John the Baptist (Mark 6:20); King Benjamin (Words of Mormon 1:17); Nephi, Sam, Jacob, and Joseph (Alma 3:6); Alma (Alma 10:7–9); Abel (Moses 5:26); and the quorum of three presidents anciently (D&C 107:29). Lest I be wrongly accused of bias, the scriptures also mention holy women: "For after this manner in the old time the holy women also, who trusted in God, adorned themselves" (1 Peter 3:5). In fact, I think we are far more likely to find a holy woman than a holy man.

I am fascinated with the concept of becoming a holy man. Although I feel I am far from it, my desire is to become such a man. It is clear from the following scriptures that God wants us to become holy. "But as he which hath called you is holy, so be ye holy in all manner of conversation; Because it is written, Be ye holy; for I am holy" (1 Peter 1:15–16). "And let every man esteem his brother as himself, and practise virtue and holiness before me" (D&C 38:24). "For God hath not called us unto uncleanness, but unto holiness" (1 Thessalonians 4:7). And finally, "Follow peace with all men, and holiness, without which no man shall see the Lord" (Hebrews 12:14).

Our body is the temple of God. As Paul taught, "If any man defile the temple of God, him shall God destroy; for the temple of God is holy, which temple ye are" (1 Corinthians 3:16–17). We are to "cleanse ourselves from all filthiness of the flesh and spirit, perfecting holiness in the fear of God" (2 Corinthians 7:1). Collectively, we must seek for holiness, "For Zion must increase in beauty, and in holiness; her borders must be enlarged; her stakes must be strengthened; yea, verily I say unto you, Zion must arise and put on her beautiful garments" (D&C 82:14).

To be holy means to be in a state of spiritual life, godliness, innocence, and virtue. Sanctification is the process through which a person becomes holy. Moroni invited us:

> Yea, come unto Christ, and be perfected in him, and *deny yourselves of all ungodliness*; and if ye shall deny yourselves of all ungodliness, and love God with all your might, mind and strength, then is his grace sufficient for you, that by his grace ye may be perfect in Christ; and if by the grace of God ye are perfect in Christ, ye can in nowise deny the power of God.
>
> And again, if ye by the grace of God are perfect in Christ, and

> deny not his power, then are ye sanctified in Christ by the grace of God, through the shedding of the blood of Christ, which is in the covenant of the Father unto the remission of your sins, *that ye become holy, without spot*. (Moroni 10:32–33, emphasis added)

Part of becoming holy is denying ourselves of all ungodliness. We must try do this ourselves through self-discipline, but in the end, it is the Lord Jesus Christ who has the power to make us holy: "For I am able to make you holy, and your sins are forgiven you" (D&C 60:7).

FROM WICKED TO HOLY IN TEN YEARS

Let's look at an example in the life of one of the holy men mentioned above—Alma the Younger. In 92 BC, Alma was described as follows: "Now the sons of Mosiah were numbered among the unbelievers; and also one of the sons of Alma was numbered among them, he being called Alma, after his father; nevertheless, *he became a very wicked and an idolatrous man*. And he was a man of many words, and did speak much flattery to the people; therefore he led many of the people to do after the manner of his iniquities" (Mosiah 27:8, emphasis added).

Ten years later, in 82 BC, the following description was given of this same Alma:

> As I was journeying to see a very near kindred, behold an angel of the Lord appeared unto me and said: Amulek, return to thine own house, for thou shalt feed *a prophet of the Lord*; yea, *a holy man*, who is *a chosen man of God*; for he has fasted many days because of the sins of this people, and he is an hungered, and thou shalt receive him into thy house and feed him, and he shall bless thee and thy house; and the blessing of the Lord shall rest upon thee and thy house.
>
> And it came to pass that I obeyed the voice of the angel, and returned towards my house. And as I was going thither I found the man whom the angel said unto me: Thou shalt receive into thy house—and behold it was this same man who has been speaking unto you concerning the things of God.
>
> *And the angel said unto me he is a holy man; wherefore I know he is a holy man* because it was said by an angel of God. (Alma 10:7–9; emphasis added)

In 92 BC, Alma was a wicked and idolatrous man. Ten years later, he had repented of his sins, and the Lord had washed him clean through the Atonement. He had been sanctified and had become a holy man. Isn't it encouraging to know that a person can go from wicked to holy in just ten years or less? With God, nothing is impossible.

The Challenge of Our Times

I have often thought I would not have been a very good Mormon pioneer. I'm not much of an outdoorsman, unless you count a golf course (which has been thoroughly sprayed for bugs) as the outdoors. I honor my pioneer heritage and give thanks for those who demonstrated such courage and faithfulness. As they wended their way toward their refuge in the Rocky Mountains, they had many daunting challenges, including suffering and fleeing persecution for their religious beliefs and burying their children in shallow graves.

It seems to me that our challenge, in our time, is different but still daunting—to strive to be holy in an unholy world. Things that would have been shameful in years past are now done openly with perverse pride. One of my friends worked for a major corporation with a flamboyant billionaire CEO. It was not unusual for a female employee to bring a sexual harassment lawsuit against the company, based on the CEO's inappropriate behavior. Privately this CEO laughed and said that because he was a billionaire, he could do anything he wanted. If a woman complained, he would simply give her a million-dollar settlement, which was like pennies to him. In his mind, his wealth made him invincible.

Some surveys have shown that 90 percent of men who travel regularly on business are unfaithful to their wives. The media—books, magazines, movies, television, and music—are full of unclean and unholy acts and images. It is hard to keep our minds clean in today's environment. Years ago, I worked at a large high-tech company and was responsible for the legal and security functions. This was in the early days of the Internet, when it was not as pervasive as it is today. I asked the head of security to check our employees' use of the Internet during business hours over a two-week period, not keeping track of employee names. He sadly reported to me that eighteen of every twenty Internet hits during business hours were on pornographic or similar sites.

There is no doubt that it will take our best personal effort to become a holy person in an unholy world. We will need to watch what we allow to enter our homes, hearts, and minds. We will need to "let virtue garnish [our] thoughts unceasingly" (D&C 121:45). Ultimately, it is God who will make us holy (D&C 60:7), but only if we try our best over a long period of time to keep the commandments and to think noble and uplifting thoughts. It will be a constant challenge, and it will require much repentance, but we need to rise to the challenge of our time. We will need to pray for the help so beautifully described in the third verse of the hymn "More Holiness Give Me,"

More purity give me,
More strength to o'ercome
More freedom from earth-stains,
More longing for home.
More fit for the kingdom,
More used would I be,
More blessed and holy—
More, Savior, like thee.[2]

Godliness

Closely related to holiness is the concept of godliness. President George Q. Cannon said:

> It should be the aim of every Latter-day Saint to be godly, to understand godliness, and to carry out godliness in his or her life, so that we all shall be like our Father in heaven as near as we possibly can be. Jesus has given us to understand that it is possible for His disciples to be perfect. . . . He did not mean by that that we should attain to the fulness of godhood in this life, but that we should carry out in our lives and exemplify in our conduct those laws and principles which God has revealed and which are the principles of perfection and godliness.[3]

Godliness is one of the divine virtues listed by the Apostle Peter (2 Peter 1:7–8). Men of corrupt minds mistakenly suppose that "gain is godliness" (1 Timothy 6:5–6). But the man of God is to follow after righteousness and godliness (1 Timothy 6:11). God has given unto us "all things that pertain unto life and godliness, through the knowledge of him that hath called us to glory and virtue" (2 Peter 1:3).

As a person who exercises, but doesn't necessarily like it, the following scripture rings true: "But refuse profane and old wives' fables, and exercise thyself rather unto godliness. *For bodily exercise profiteth little: but godliness is profitable unto all things*, having promise of the life that now is, and of that which is to come" (1 Timothy 4:7–8. emphasis added).

"Cleanliness is next to godliness" is a well-known American proverb. I understand that a clean body and living environment are important, but I have wondered whether such cleanliness is really next to godliness. Recently a friend pointed out to me that it's possible to consider this proverb in another light, for the scriptures teach that no unclean thing can enter into the kingdom of God (see 3 Nephi 27:19; 1 Nephi 10:21; Alma 11:37; Alma 40:26). Cleanliness in a moral sense really is next to godliness.

Honesty as a Part of Godliness

One important aspect of godliness is honesty. As a lawyer I have been involved in international business for more than twenty-five years. Many of the people I have associated with have been men and women of honesty and integrity. But surprisingly, I have witnessed close up many business people whom I would not consider honest. Sadly, some of these people consider themselves good and religious people. But they are able to partition their religious life from their business life. Church is one thing; business is another. Somehow, in their minds, they are able to convince themselves that they are honest, when in matters of business they most definitely are not. These things ought not to be. We should have the integrity to be the same honest person seven days a week, twenty-four hours a day, no matter what the context. For "what manner of persons ought [we] to be in all holy conversation and godliness?" (2 Peter 3:11).

Interestingly, some people who are truly religious and honest believe that their righteousness should somehow lead directly to financial prosperity. Just like those whose minds are corrupt, they mistakenly think that "gain is godliness" (1 Timothy 6:5), which most assuredly is not true.

The Mystery of Godliness

One aspect of godliness is that it describes what God is like. We probably will not be able to understand this fully during our motal lives: "For, behold, the mystery of godliness, how great is it!" (D&C 19:10; 1 Timothy 3:16). However, through the ordinances of the priesthood, including the temple ordinances, we will sense the power of godliness: "Therefore, in the ordinances thereof, the power of godliness is manifest. And without the ordinances thereof, and the authority of the priesthood, the power of godliness is not manifest unto men in the flesh" (D&C 84:20–21).

To put things in perspective, the Prophet Joseph said, "Search your hearts, and see if you are like God. I have searched mine, and feel to repent of all my sins."[4]

Virtue

"We believe in being *honest, true, chaste, benevolent, virtuous*, and in doing good to all men" (Articles of Faith 1:13, emphasis added). Virtue, which includes chastity, is an important aspect of holiness and godliness. Every man should "esteem his brother as himself, and practise virtue and holiness before [the Lord]" (D&C 38:24). We are to "let virtue garnish [our] thoughts unceasingly" (D&C 121:45) and to "walk in the paths of virtue" (D&C 25:2). "Who can find a virtuous woman? For her price is far above rubies" (Proverbs 31:10). The same thing could be said of a virtuous man. We should ask ourselves whether we love virtue, for "virtue loveth virtue" (D&C 88:40).

Virtue is synonymous with chastity. The law of chastity is under assault in our modern world. Much of the world has given up on the institution of marriage. At least half of all marriages end in divorce, often because of infidelity.

As of today, I have been a bishop three different times for a total of more than eleven years. I have spent many, many hours hearing tear-filled confessions of members concerning violations of the law of chastity. I heard other confessions as a mission president, from missionaries who either failed to be fully honest with their bishop and stake president before their mission or who committed a sin while serving their mission. It is obvious to me that it is hard to live the law of chastity in an unholy and unchaste world.

Someone who has broken the law of chastity and has not fully repented is not in a state of holiness, godliness, or virtue. Thankfully, through the application of the Atonement of Jesus Christ, repentance and cleansing are possible. I am a witness of this, having helped many members apply the Atonement in their lives to repent of sexual sin.

I will never forget the experience of a young woman in my BYU ward who had committed a series of serious sexual sins. Her repentance process was fairly long and arduous. She completely turned her life around and, for many months, prayed for forgiveness. Her *modus operandi* was to jog up by the Provo Temple, find a quiet spot in the trees behind the temple, and pray, asking for forgiveness. As she prayed, she usually was so sad that projectile tears flew out from her eyes.

One evening she burst into my office unannounced, wearing her jogging clothes, interrupting another appointment for a few moments, to tell me that there had been a difference in her prayer that evening. She had prayed, but there were no more tears. Instead, her soul felt nothing but happiness and peace. "Am I forgiven?" she asked. We read together from the Book of Mormon: "And it came to pass that after they had spoken these words the Spirit of the Lord came upon them, and they were *filled with joy*, having received a remission of their sins, and having *peace of conscience*, because of the exceeding faith which they had in Jesus Christ" (Mosiah 4:3; emphasis added). Counseling together, we decided that she had received a remission of her sins because of her faith in Jesus Christ, and that it was time for her to have a limited-use temple recommend and all the other privileges of membership in the Church.

The hope that repentance brings is magnificent and real. However, it's always better to avoid the sin in the first place. As discussed above, this requires self-discipline. It involves thinking virtuous thoughts, doing virtuous actions, and standing in holy places.

Conclusion

We live in an unholy world. Somehow we are to become holy, godly, and virtuous. Jesus Christ has the power to make us holy but will only do so as we deny ourselves of ungodliness and strive to live in a holy and virtuous manner, repenting as necessary along the way. Becoming holy truly is possible—and what hope and peace this gives us.

Summary

- Holiness and godliness mean saintly, godly, pious, devout, and religious. Virtue means moral excellence, goodness, purity, and integrity.

- There are a number of men and women in the scriptures who were called "holy."
- Sanctification is the process through which a person becomes holy.
- Part of becoming holy is denying ourselves of ungodliness. This we do through self-discipline.
- In the end, Jesus has the power to make us holy.
- Alma the Younger went from wicked to holy in under ten years.
- One of the challenges of our time is trying to be holy in an unholy world. We need to watch carefully what we allow to enter our homes, hearts, and minds.
- It should be the aim of every Latter-day Saint to be godly. Cleanliness in the moral sense really is next to godliness.
- Honesty is an aspect of godliness. A godly person cannot partition his business life from his religious life. We must be honest in all areas of our life.
- Gain is not godliness.
- The mystery of godliness (what God is like) is great, but we gain glimpses through the ordinances of the priesthood.
- Virtue is synonymous with chastity. The law of chastity is under assault in our modern world. It is difficult to keep the law of chastity in our unholy world, but it is possible. Those who sin can be forgiven through the Atonement.
- Jesus has the power to make us holy as we deny ourselves of ungodliness and strive to live in a holy and virtuous manner, repenting as necessary along the way.

Notes

1. *Encyclopedia of Mormonism*, 1236.
2. *Hymns of The Church of Jesus Christ of Latter-day Saints* (Salt Lake City: The Church of Jesus Christ of Latter-day Saints, 1985), no. 131.
3. Cannon, *Gospel Truth*, vol. 1, 22.
4. Joseph Smith, *History of The Church of Jesus Christ of Latter-day Saints*, vol. 4, 588.

12

Knowledge

Of all the treasures of knowledge, the most truly vital is the knowledge of God, of his existence, his powers, his love, and his promises. Through this knowledge, we learn that our great objective in life is to build character. In fact, we learn that the building of faith and character is paramount, for character is higher than intellect, and perfect character will be continually rewarded with increased intellect.

Thus, our real business on earth is to master self. And as we master ourselves, we will learn to master the earth and its elements. Most important, we will learn how to help others overcome and perfect themselves in all ways of living.

—*Spencer W. Kimball*[1]

As a bishop, I attend the priest quorum, where each Sunday we stand and state the purposes of the Aaronic Priesthood, including: "Obtain as much education as possible." Once in awhile I jokingly remind the young men that this statement is only true to a point—about the time they're working on their second PhD, their wife will probably let them know it's time to get a job.

Still, knowledge is one of the divine virtues (2 Peter 1:5). And knowledge and wisdom are gifts of the spirit, "For to one is given by the Spirit the *word of wisdom*; to another the *word of knowledge* by the same Spirit" (1 Corinthians 12:8; see also D&C 46:17–18, emphasis added).

Moroni explains, "For behold, to one is given by the Spirit of God, that he may *teach the word of wisdom*; And to another, that he may *teach the word of knowledge* by the same Spirit" (Moroni 10:9–10, emphasis added).

In 2 Peter, where many of the divine virtues are enumerated, the concluding verse says that "if these things be in you, and abound, they make you that ye shall neither be barren nor unfruitful in the *knowledge of our Lord Jesus Christ*" (2 Peter 1:8, emphasis added). In other words, if we take upon ourselves the divine virtues, we will be fruitful in our knowledge of the Lord Jesus Christ. And, while the knowledge referred to in the scriptures applies to both spiritual and temporal knowledge, "true knowledge . . . is the knowledge of [our] Redeemer" (Helaman 15:13; see also Jacob 4:12).

Knowledge of Spiritual and Temporal Things

The main focus of this chapter, therefore, is knowledge of spiritual things. However, it is worth noting that God desires us to be learned in temporal things as well. If that were not true, the Church would not spend the amount of money it does on Brigham Young University and its affiliated campuses. The main purpose of these schools is to teach the knowledge of the world in a setting of faith. In the Doctrine and Covenants, we learn of the importance of obtaining knowledge:

> Teach ye diligently and my grace shall attend you, that you may be instructed more perfectly in theory, in principle, in doctrine, in the law of the gospel, in all things that pertain unto the kingdom of God, that are expedient for you to understand;
>
> Of things both in heaven and in the earth, and under the earth; things which have been, things which are, things which must shortly come to pass; things which are at home, things which are abroad; the wars and the perplexities of the nations, and the judgments which are on the land; and a knowledge also of countries and of kingdoms. (D&C 88:78–79)

This scripture is broad enough to include knowledge of God and spiritual things as well as knowledge of man and temporal things, including geology, history, current events, law, foreign affairs, and politics.

The Lord also said: "And, verily I say unto you, that it is my will that you should hasten to translate my *scriptures*, and to obtain a *knowledge of history*, and of *countries*, and of *kingdoms*, of *laws* of God and man, and all this for the salvation of Zion" (D&C 93:53, emphasis added). Once again, we are to obtain knowledge of the scriptures and laws of God, as well as the history and laws of man.

As we follow the Lord's counsel to obtain temporal learning, we need to do so with a degree of caution, for "knowledge puffeth up, but charity edifieth" (1 Corinthians 8:1). There is a risk that knowledge will lead to pride. We must not be "ever learning, and never able to come to the knowledge of the truth" (2 Timothy 3:7).

Nephi warned, "O that cunning plan of the evil one! O the vainness, and the frailties, and the foolishness of men! *When they are learned they think they are wise*, and they hearken not unto the counsel of God, for they set it aside, *supposing they know of themselves*, wherefore, their wisdom is foolishness and it profiteth them not. And they shall perish. *But to be learned is good if they hearken unto the counsels of God*" (2 Nephi 9:28–29, emphasis added).

"Charity never faileth," but "whether there be knowledge, it shall vanish away" (1 Corinthians 13:8). We must keep this in mind: "And though I have the gift of prophecy, and *understand all mysteries, and all knowledge*; and though I have all faith, so that I could remove mountains, and have not charity, I am nothing" (1 Corinthians 13:2, emphasis added).

So do we have any shining examples of knowledge *with* charity? There are many, but one who springs immediately to mind is Elder Dallin H. Oaks. Elder Oaks has one of the finest legal minds in the nation. In my opinion, he is qualified to serve as a U.S. Supreme Court Justice. If he were in private practice, he would make a fortune. And yet, with all his learning and legal sophistication, he is a humble servant of God. He hearkens to the counsel of the Lord. He is a man of good humor and good will. He has not forgotten that without charity he is nothing. These words of James describe Elder Oaks: "Who is a wise man and endued with knowledge among you? Let him shew out of a good conversation his works with meekness of wisdom" (James 3:13).

There are three final points regarding knowledge of the world: First, it is clear we should continue to learn and grow throughout our lives. However, it is my experience that, as a general rule, the time for formal education is when we are young. I have known a fair number of young people who decided to work full-time and go to school part-time. This is not, in my opinion, a formula for educational success, because these young people often get distracted and never finish their formal education. I believe a young person should get his or her education before obtaining a full-time position. In my view, it is best to go straight through and get a degree (even an advanced degree), pausing only to serve a mission. (The mission experience makes a person a better student.)

There may be a situation where pausing may be beneficial. I have heard it may be best to get a bachelor's degree, work for a while, and then obtain a masters in business administration. But generally, I think it's a risk to take a full-time job before completing one's formal education.

Second, we should continue to seek knowledge throughout our lives, even long after our formal education has been completed. My ward recently celebrated the ninetieth birthday of a most remarkable woman, Betsey Williams. A reception was held in the Primary room, but our Relief Society president completely transformed the room so that it appeared nothing like a Primary room. It was filled with beautiful things Betsey had created: a dress she made from silk she acquired on a visit to China; a teakettle she pounded from a flat sheet of brass; an oil painting she painted; scale models she made of her childhood home and the home in which she raised her children; a book she wrote and bound; and many other beautiful things she has made.

Betsey is from Maine. She is an educated and proper woman. She still has a Maine accent—almost, but not quite, a British accent. Betsey is very active. She walks each day with several sisters in the ward. She is a diligent student of the scriptures. She heads up a book club that meets monthly at her home. If you agree to moderate a club meeting on a particular book, Betsey contacts you about a week in advance with information that will help you lead the discussion. She fills her days with meaningful work, study, and service.

Betsey is president of our Gospel Doctrine class. She starts each class with a brief but well-thought-out introduction. Not long ago, for more than a year, she served as our Primary Achievement Day leader. She told me she had enough energy to do it for about a year. Betsey was completely devoted to this calling. Her strong testimony and amazing creativity made a lasting impact on the young girls she served. Can you just imagine it—the relationship developed between an eleven-year-old girl and an eighty-nine-year-old loving, dignified, creative, faithful woman? It was wonderful.

The third and final point is this: apparently persons who are truly knowledgeable tend not to be overly talkative. In Proverbs we read: "He that hath knowledge spareth his words: and a man of understanding is of an excellent spirit. Even a fool, when he holdeth his peace, is counted wise: and he that shutteth his lips is esteemed a man of understanding" (Proverbs 17:27–28). Or, in today's parlance, "It is better to remain silent and be thought a fool than to open one's mouth and remove all doubt."

Spiritual Knowledge

Turning now to knowledge in the spiritual sense, we are to strive to gain knowledge of God (see Mosiah 18:26), of the Redeemer (see 1 Nephi 15:14; 2 Nephi 10:2; Mosiah 27:36), and of the truth (see Helaman 15:6–7; Alma 17:2; Mosiah 27:36). The Proverb says, "Apply thine heart unto instruction, and thine ears to the words of knowledge" (Proverbs 23:12). God is the fountain of all wisdom and knowledge. No one can "teach God knowledge" (Job 21:22), for God is "perfect in knowledge" (Job 37:16).

When young Jesus went missing on the way home from Jerusalem, Mary and Joseph eventually found him engaged in the pursuit of knowledge: "And it came to pass, that after three days they found him in the temple, sitting in the midst of the doctors, both hearing them, and asking them questions. And all that heard him were astonished at his understanding and answers" (Luke 2:46–47).

It was not possible for lawyers or other learned persons of the day to "trap" Jesus, for He was masterful in His knowledge of the scriptures, not to mention the intent of their hearts. As He walked along the road to Emmaus, "beginning at Moses and all the prophets, he expounded unto them in all the scriptures the things concerning himself" (Luke 24:27; see also 3 Nephi 23:6, 14).

No doubt much of Jesus' knowledge came from revelation, for He too was a prophet. But we know this from latter-day revelation: "And I, John, saw that [Jesus] received not of the fulness at the first, but received grace for grace; And he received not of the fulness at first, but continued from grace to grace, until he received a fulness; And thus he was called the Son of God, because he received not of the fulness at the first" (D&C 93:12–14).

I think it fair to say that one source of Jesus' knowledge was good old-fashioned study. Experience also helped, as He continued from grace to grace. We too will need personal revelation and study to obtain knowledge, ripening to wisdom, as we grow line upon line, precept upon precept, from grace to grace.

Jesus said, "Learn of me, and listen to my words; walk in the meekness of my Spirit, and you shall have peace in me" (D&C 19:23). The ambiguous nature of prepositions gives this teaching a possible dual meaning. Learning *of* Him can mean learning *from* Him; it can also mean learning *about* Him. There can be no better way to learn knowledge and wisdom than from the teachings of Jesus and by studying about His life and following His example.

We know that "the glory of God is intelligence, or, in other words, light and truth (D&C 93:36). And we know that "it is impossible for a man to be saved in ignorance" (D&C 131:6). In fact, "a man is saved no faster than he gets knowledge."[2] There are many things I love about the gospel, but one aspect that I particularly like is that it is simple enough that a child eight years of age can understand its basics sufficiently to make the baptismal covenant, but it is so rich and deep in meaning that it warrants a lifetime of study, and beyond.

There is, however, a major difference between the quest for gospel knowledge and testimony, on the one hand, and scientific or worldly learning, on the other. Elder Dallin H. Oaks has helpfully explained,

> What do we mean when we testify and say that we know the gospel is true? Contrast that kind of knowledge with "I know it is cold outside" or "I know I love my wife." These are three different kinds of knowledge, each learned in a different way. Knowledge of outside temperature can be verified by scientific proof. Knowledge that we love our spouse is personal and subjective. While not capable of scientific proof, it is still important. *The idea that all important knowledge is based on scientific evidence is simply untrue.*
>
> While there are some "evidences" for gospel truths (for example, see Psalm 19:1; Helaman 8:24), scientific methods will not yield spiritual knowledge. This is what Jesus taught in response to Simon Peter's testimony that He was the Christ: "Blessed art thou, Simon

> Bar-jona: for flesh and blood hath not revealed it unto thee, but my Father which is in heaven" (Matthew 16:17). The Apostle Paul explained this. In a letter to the Corinthian Saints, he said, "The things of God knoweth no man, but [by] the Spirit of God" (1 Corinthians 2:11; see also John 14:17).[3]

How to Learn Spiritual Knowledge

With this backdrop, let us look at what the scriptures teach about the various ways to learn knowledge and wisdom of God. In Proverbs, we read that "the fear of the Lord is the beginning of knowledge" (Proverbs 1:7). In this sense "fear does not mean that we are afraid of the Lord. According to the Bible Dictionary, "The 'fear of the Lord' is frequently spoken of as part of man's duty . . . and is also described as 'godly fear.' In such passages fear is equivalent to reverence, awe, worship, and is therefore an essential part of the attitude of mind in which we ought to stand toward the All-holy God" (Bible Dictionary, "Fear," 672). So our starting point in acquiring spiritual knowledge is a reverent and worshipful attitude toward God.

Related to this spirit of reverence is our own sense of humility, for as we are taught in latter-day revelation, "And inasmuch as they were humble they might be made strong, and blessed from on high, and *receive knowledge from time to time*" (D&C 1:28, emphasis added). The Doctrine and Covenants also tells us, "Let him that is ignorant learn *wisdom by humbling himself* and calling upon the Lord his God, that his eyes may be opened that he may see, and his ears opened that he may hear" (D&C 136:32, emphasis added). Spiritual things are not learned by the arrogant. Usually, the arrogant don't even try to learn.

With a humble heart, we ask the Lord in faith to give us spiritual knowledge. Abraham desired to "to be one who possessed great knowledge" and "to possess a greater knowledge" (Abraham 1:2). Solomon sought (and was blessed with) wisdom and knowledge so he could properly judge his people; he did not ask for riches, wealth, or honor, but was given these things as well (see 2 Chronicles 1:9–12). Likewise, we should ask for knowledge: "Oliver Cowdery [or insert your own name], verily, verily, I say unto you, that assuredly as the Lord liveth, who is your God and your Redeemer, *even so surely shall you receive a knowledge of whatsoever things you shall ask in faith, with an honest heart, believing that you shall receive*" (D&C 8:1, emphasis added).

We also learn, "*If thou shalt ask, thou shalt receive revelation upon revelation, knowledge upon knowledge, that thou mayest know the mysteries and peaceable things*—that which bringeth joy, that which bringeth life eternal" (D&C 42:61, emphasis added). We must ask in faith, with an honest heart, believing we will receive. President George Q. Cannon said that "faith lies at the foundation of our religion, and it is impossible to grow in a knowledge of the truth or to please God without it."[4]

Having asked in faith, we need to be obedient. "But if they obey not . . . they shall die without knowledge" (Job 36:12). And as Jesus taught: "If any man will do his will, he shall know of the doctrine, whether it be of God, or whether I speak of myself" (John 7:17). Personal righteousness flowing from obedience opens the door to spiritual knowledge. Alma taught: "O, remember, my son, and learn wisdom in thy youth; yea, learn in thy youth to keep the commandments of God" (Alma 37:35).

According to the Prophet Joseph Smith, failure to obey leads to a loss of knowledge: "As far as we degenerate from God, we descend to the devil and lose knowledge, and without knowledge we cannot be saved, and while our hearts are filled with evil, and we are studying evil, there is no room in our hearts for good, or studying good. Is not God good? Then you be good; if He is faithful, then you be faithful. Add to your faith virtue, to virtue knowledge, and seek for every good thing."[5]

Study is an important aspect of the acquisition of knowledge: "And as all have not faith, seek ye diligently and teach one another words of wisdom; yea, seek ye out of the best books words of wisdom; seek learning, even by study and also by faith" (D&C 88:118). In this regard, there are many wonderful books, but there are no more important books than the scriptures. And we, as Latter-day Saints, are blessed to have additional scriptures that amplify and lend support to the teachings of the Bible. Foremost among these latter-day scriptures is the Book of Mormon. Of the Book of Mormon, the Doctrine and Covenants says that just as "the knowledge of a Savior has come unto the world, through the testimony of the Jews" (D&C 3:16), the Book of Mormon will come forth "that the Lamanites might come to the knowledge of their fathers, and that they might know the promises of the Lord, and that they may believe the gospel and rely upon the merits of Jesus Christ, and be glorified through faith in his name, and that through their repentance they might be saved" (D&C 3:20).

Serious scripture study will help us "wax strong in the knowledge of the truth," as we learn from the happy reunion of Alma and his brethren, the sons of Mosiah: "Now these sons of Mosiah were with Alma at the time the angel first appeared unto him; therefore Alma did rejoice exceedingly to see his brethren; and what added more to his joy, they were still his brethren in the Lord; yea, and they had waxed strong in the knowledge of the truth; for they were men of a sound understanding and they had searched the scriptures diligently, that they might know the word of God" (Alma 17:2, emphasis added).

In addition to obtaining knowledge from the best books, we can learn from teachers, especially those who teach with the Spirit. In the Doctrine and Covenants, we are instructed: "Teach ye diligently and my grace shall attend you, that you may be instructed more perfectly in theory, in principle, in doctrine, in the law of the gospel, in all things that pertain unto the kingdom of God, that are expedient for you to understand" (D&C 88:78). Some of our dear brothers and sisters have the spiritual gift to "teach the word of wisdom" and to "teach the word of knowledge" (Moroni 10:9–10). We can avail ourselves of seminary and institute, Gospel Doctrine class, and inspired speakers during general and stake conferences and weekly sacrament meetings. As Paul said: "And he gave some, apostles; and some, prophets; and some, evangelists; and some, pastors and teachers; For the perfecting of the saints, for the work of the ministry, *for the edifying of the body of Christ*: Till we all come in the unity of the faith, and *of the knowledge of the Son of God*, unto a perfect man, unto the measure of the stature of the fulness of Christ" (Ephesians 4:11–13, emphasis added).

A key to the knowledge of the mysteries of God lies in the greater priesthood and the temple ordinances. As we qualify to go to the temple and participate in temple ordinances, first for ourselves and then for others, we will learn the mysteries of the kingdom: "And this greater priesthood administereth the gospel and holdeth the key of the mysteries of the kingdom, even the key of the knowledge of God. Therefore, in the ordinances thereof, the power of godliness is manifest. And without the ordinances thereof, and the authority of the priesthood, the power of godliness is not manifest unto men in the flesh" (D&C 84:19–21).

When we keep the Word of Wisdom, we are promised health benefits, but also, even more important, "wisdom and great treasures of knowledge, even hidden treasures" (D&C 89:18–19). This is because a clean, clear-thinking, non-addicted, and healthy body is a better receptacle of the Spirit of the Holy Ghost. Such a physical body is better able to feel and recognize personal revelation.

Spiritual knowledge comes through the Holy Ghost: "God shall give unto you knowledge by his Holy Spirit, yea, by the unspeakable gift of the Holy Ghost, that has not been revealed since the world was until now" (D&C 121:26). And Paul said: "For what man knoweth the things of a man, save the spirit of man which is in him? even so the things of God knoweth no man, but the Spirit of God" (1 Corinthians 2:11). In the Book of Mormon, Ammon spoke of his calling to teach and explained how he had obtained his knowledge. "Ammon said unto him: I am a man; and man in the beginning was created after the image of God, and I am called by his *Holy Spirit* to teach these things unto this people, that they may be brought to a knowledge of that which is just and true; *And a portion of that Spirit dwelleth in me, which giveth me knowledge*, and also power according to my faith and desires which are in God" (Alma 18:34–35, emphasis added).

We will learn spiritual knowledge little by little, over a long period of time. We cannot know things all at once, but "must grow in grace and in the knowledge of the truth" (D&C 50:40).

In summary, then, the scriptures teach that we learn knowledge of spiritual things by:

1. Fearing God, or having a feeling of reverence and awe toward Him.
2. Striving to have a humble heart.
3. Asking in faith, with an honest heart, believing we will receive.
4. Obeying the commandments and developing personal righteousness.
5. Studying and seeking wisdom from the best books, especially the scriptures.
6. Being taught by inspired teachers who have the spirit of God with them.
7. Attending the temple and participating in temple ordinances

performed by the higher priesthood.
8. Keeping the Word of Wisdom.
9. Receiving revelation through the Holy Ghost.
10. Patiently remembering that knowledge comes little by little as we grow in grace and in the knowledge of the truth.

God Will Give Us Knowledge

The knowledge that is of most value is knowledge that leads to salvation and exaltation. "Truth is knowledge of things as they are, and as they were, and as they are to come" (D&C 93:24). God is anxious to share this and other knowledge with His faithful children: "How long can rolling waters remain impure? What power shall stay the heavens? As well might man stretch forth his puny arm to stop the Missouri river in its decreed course, or to turn it up stream, as to hinder the Almighty from pouring down knowledge from heaven upon the heads of the Latter-day Saints" (D&C 121:33).

Subjects of Little Consequence

Part of the purpose of life, though, is to learn to do things on our own, to become capable and independent. As some things are more important than others, we need to use good sense in inquiring of God. The Prophet Joseph taught that "it is a great thing to inquire at the hands of God or to come into his presence; and we feel fearful to approach him on subjects that are of little or no consequence."[6]

Knowledge Needed to Fulfill Our Callings

We should, of course, seek for knowledge in fulfilling our callings. Consider this good example from the journal of the Prophet Joseph: "Monday, December 21, 1835—Spent this day at home, endeavoring to treasure up knowledge for the benefit of my calling."[7] And again from the Prophet Joseph, "A man of God should be endowed with wisdom, knowledge, and understanding, in order to teach and lead the people of God."[8]

Our modern-world is full of time-wasting activities. We ought to discipline ourselves to spend a fair amount of our time in the pursuit of knowledge. "Whatever principle of intelligence we attain unto in this life, it will rise with us in the resurrection. And if a person gains more knowledge and intelligence in this life through his diligence and obedience than another, he will have so much the advantage in the world to come" (D&C 130:18–19).

Daily Sacred Grove Experience

In 2003, Elder Yoshihiko Kikuchi of the Seventy visited our mission in Korea and greatly blessed the lives of our 135 missionaries. He bore a powerful witness of the Prophet Joseph Smith and taught the missionaries how to teach the First Vision to their investigators. He also taught the missionaries (and the mission president and his wife) the concept of a daily Sacred Grove experience. Just as Joseph read the scriptures (in particular, James 1:5–6) and then went into the grove of trees to pray, we can have a daily Sacred Grove experience by studying and pondering the scriptures and praying.

We can do this even if we don't have a grove handy by identifying our own special places where we can read the scriptures and pray. Elder Kikuchi even keeps a picture of the Sacred Grove in his pocket to remind him of the importance of this concept. I have discovered that there is no better way to grow in gospel knowledge than to consistently have a daily Sacred Grove experience.

Conclusion

Gaining knowledge of the world and of God is an important purpose of this life. But I greatly appreciate the enthusiastic focus of the Apostle Paul, who said, "I count all things but loss for the excellency of the *knowledge of Christ Jesus my Lord*: for whom I have suffered the loss of all things, and do count them but dung, that I may win Christ" (Philippians 3:8, emphasis added).

Summary

- Knowledge is one of the divine attributes, and it is also a gift of the Spirit.
- We are to seek for knowledge of spiritual and temporal things.
- In seeking knowledge of temporal things, we need to be careful, for "knowledge puffeth up, but charity edifieth." We must avoid

the temptation to become proud because of our knowledge.

- It is possible to be learned and still humble and full of charity. Elder Dallin H. Oaks is a good example.
- In a spiritual sense, we are to seek knowledge of God, of the Redeemer, and of the truth.
- Jesus sought knowledge by revelation, but it is probable that He also was a good student of the scriptures.
- It is important for us to learn of Jesus—to learn *from* Him and to learn *about* Him.
- The glory of God is intelligence. It is impossible to be saved in ignorance.
- Scientific methods will not yield spiritual knowledge. We know the things of God by the Spirit of God.
- We learn of spiritual things by doing the following:

  1. Fearing God, or having a feeling of reverence and awe toward Him.
  2. Striving to have a humble heart.
  3. Asking in faith, with an honest heart, believing we will receive.
  4. Obeying the commandments and developing personal righteousness.
  5. Studying and seeking wisdom from the best books, especially the scriptures.
  6. Being taught by inspired teachers who have the spirit of God with them.
  7. Attending the temple and participating in temple ordinances performed by the higher priesthood.
  8. Keeping the Word of Wisdom.
  9. Receiving revelation through the Holy Ghost.
  10. Patiently remembering that knowledge comes little by little as we grow in grace and in the knowledge of the truth.

- The most valuable knowledge is that which leads to salvation and exaltation.
- It is a great privilege to inquire of the Lord; we should not approach Him on subjects that are of little or no consequence.
- We should seek for the knowledge needed to fulfill our callings.
- We should discipline ourselves, using our time wisely for the

purpose of gaining knowledge. If a person gains more knowledge and intelligence in this life through his or her diligence, it will be an advantage in the world to come.

- Scripture study and prayer are an important daily way to gain spiritual knowledge.

Notes

1. Spencer W. Kimball, "Seek Learning, Even by Study and Also by Faith," *Ensign*, Sept. 1983, 5.
2. Joseph Smith, *History of The Church of Jesus Christ of Latter-day Saints*, vol. 4, 588.
3. Dallin H. Oaks, "Testimony," *Ensign*, May 2008, 26–29.
4. Cannon, *Gospel Truth*, vol. 1, 149, emphasis added.
5. Joseph Smith, *History of The Church of Jesus Christ of Latter-day Saints*, vol. 4, 588.
6. Ibid., vol. 1, 339.
7. Ibid., vol. 2, 344.
8. Ibid., vol. 5, 426.

13

Mercy

How godlike a quality is mercy. It cannot be legislated. It must come from the heart. It must be stirred up from within. It is part of the endowment each of us receives as a son or daughter of God and partaker of a divine birthright. I plead for an effort among all of us to give greater expression and wider latitude to this instinct which lies within us. I am convinced that there comes a time, possibly many times, within our lives when we might cry out for mercy on the part of others. How can we expect it unless we have been merciful ourselves?

—*Gordon B. Hinckley*[1]

A WONDERFUL MAN NAMED Brother Ko served in the Korea Daejeon Stake presidency. The story I'm about to tell occurred in 2002 when the World Cup soccer tournament was held jointly in Korea and Japan. Like all Koreans, Brother Ko loved soccer, and so did his teenaged son. And like all teenagers, his son sometimes gave Brother Ko trouble.

Although I'm no expert at soccer (baseball's my game), I understand that in soccer there are yellow cards and red cards. The yellow card is thrown when a player commits a foul and is a cautionary warning or a temporary suspension. If the player commits a serious violation, the referee throws the red card, meaning the player is permanently ejected from the game.

Around this time that the World Cup was going on, Brother Ko's son made a terrible mistake. Brother Ko was angry, so he called his son in to speak with him and said, "For what you have done, I'm throwing the yellow card. If you ever do it, or anything like it again, I'm throwing the red card and sending you away to the countryside to live and work." His son was duly sad and went to his room.

His heart began to soften when he saw his son's sadness, and Brother Ko pondered his use of the yellow/red card analogy. He realized that in his life he had made many mistakes (like all of us) and that God had thrown the yellow card on him, but never the red card. He went to his son and humbly asked his forgiveness for being too harsh. He told his son, "Because I love you, I will always throw the yellow card on you whenever you do something seriously wrong, for I want the best for you. But, as God has never thrown the red card on me, I will always have hope and love for you, and I will never throw the red card on you."

God and Jesus Are Merciful

If there is one thing that is clear about God, it is that He is merciful, much more so than a soccer referee. He will throw the yellow card, but He rarely throws the red card. We can trust in His mercy (see Psalm 13:5). In fact, we can "be glad and rejoice in [His] mercy." (Psalm 31:7) We can also have hope in His mercy (see Psalm 33:18).

President George Q. Cannon taught this principle beautifully: "I can say for the encouragement of all who are struggling that God is very, very merciful. He is willing to forgive all who come unto Him in humility."[2] President Cannon used the word *very* twice in describing God's mercy. God is not only merciful, He's very, very merciful.

The Book of Mormon puts it this way: "Behold, I would exhort you that when ye shall read these things . . . that *ye would remember how merciful the Lord hath been unto the children of men,* from the creation of Adam even down until the time that ye shall receive these things, and ponder it in your hearts" (Moroni 10:3, emphasis added).

I love the Pearl of Great Price because it allows us to get to know Enoch better. But it also lets us get to know God better as well. Enoch was shocked when he witnessed God, the greatest of all, weeping over the wickedness of some of the people. A poignant conversation followed.

> And it came to pass that the God of heaven looked upon the residue of the people, and he wept; and Enoch bore record of it,

> saying: How is it that the heavens weep, and shed forth their tears as the rain upon the mountains? And Enoch said unto the Lord: How is it that thou canst weep, seeing thou art holy, and from all eternity to all eternity? And were it possible that man could number the particles of the earth, yea, millions of earths like this, it would not be a beginning to the number of thy creations; and thy curtains are stretched out still; and yet thou art there, and thy bosom is there; and also thou art just; *thou art merciful and kind forever*; And thou hast taken Zion to thine own bosom, from all thy creations, from all eternity to all eternity; and naught but peace, justice, and truth is the habitation of thy throne; *and mercy shall go before thy face and have no end*; how is it thou canst weep? The Lord said unto Enoch: Behold these thy brethren; they are the workmanship of mine own hands, and I gave unto them their knowledge, in the day I created them; and in the Garden of Eden, gave I unto man his agency; And unto thy brethren have I said, and also given commandment, that they should love one another, and that they should choose me, their Father; but behold, they are without affection, and they hate their own blood. (Moses 7:28–33; emphasis added)

God wept because He loved His children and they rejected Him, did not keep His commandments, and failed to love one another.

Numerous scriptures testify of the merciful nature of God the Father and His Son Jesus Christ. "For the Lord thy God is a merciful God; he will not forsake thee" (Deuteronomy 4:31). "O give thanks unto the LORD; for he is good; for his mercy endureth for ever" (1 Chronicles 16:34). We read, "[B]ut thou art a God ready to pardon, gracious and merciful, slow to anger, and of great kindness" (Nehemiah 9:17).

We also know that "The Lord is merciful and gracious, slow to anger, and plenteous in mercy" (Psalm 103:8; Joel 2:13). And He has said, "Nevertheless, I will be merciful unto them, saith the Lord God, if they will repent and come unto me; for mine arm is lengthened out all the day long" (2 Nephi 28:32). And finally, "Behold, we count them happy which endure. Ye have heard of the patience of Job, and have seen the end of the Lord; that the Lord is very pitiful, and of tender mercy" (James 5:11).

In fact, I counted 188 scriptural verses that mention the mercy of God or Jesus—and I may have missed a few.

My wife once told me she loved certain parts of the book of Ether in the Book of Mormon but dreaded the war chapters. Then, after finishing the war chapters, she had the feeling that the message from those chapters was that God never gives up on us. In the book of Ether, God's merciful nature manifested itself in His continuing willingness to reach out toward His children, even when they were wicked.

Nothing pleases the Father more than when His children repent so that He can exercise His mercy in forgiving them. In the New Testament the Lord said: "For I will be merciful to their unrighteousness, and their sins and their iniquities will I remember no more" (Hebrews 8:12; see also D&C 58:42). What a great promise that the omniscient God will remember our sins no more!

In my research for this chapter, I read every scripture in the four standard works that includes any derivative of the word *mercy*, and in doing so one thing was clear to me: God is full of mercy for all His children, but especially for those who believe on His name, love Him, and strive to keep His commandments (see Alma 32:22; Mosiah 13:14; Exodus 20:6; Nehemiah 1:5).

For Mercy's Sake

It is for mercy's sake—to make forgiveness possible—that Jesus condescended from His throne on high to come to the earth. "And now, the *plan of mercy* could not be brought about except an atonement should be made; therefore God himself atoneth for the sins of the world, to bring about the *plan of mercy*, to appease the demands of justice, that God might be a perfect, *just God*, and a *merciful God* also" (Alma 42:15, emphasis added).

> And thus God breaketh the bands of death, having gained the victory over death; giving the Son power to make intercession for the children of men—Having ascended into heaven, having the bowels of mercy; being filled with compassion towards the children of men; standing betwixt them and justice; having broken the bands of death, taken upon himself their iniquity and their transgressions, having redeemed them, and satisfied the demands of justice. (Mosiah 15:8–9)

In 2 Nephi we read, "There is no flesh that can dwell in the presence of God, save it be through the merits, and mercy, and grace of the Holy Messiah, who layeth down his life according to the flesh, and taketh it again by the power of the Spirit, that he may bring to pass the resurrection of the dead, being the first that should rise" (2 Nephi 2:8). The plan of salvation, including the Savior's death and resurrection, is called the "merciful plan of the great Creator" (2 Nephi 9:6).

It was also for mercy's sake that the Savior healed the sick. When He visited the Nephites, He said: "Have ye any that are sick among you? Bring them hither. Have ye any that are lame, or blind, or halt, or maimed, or leprous, or that are withered, or that are deaf, or that are afflicted in any manner? Bring them hither and I will heal them, *for I have compassion upon you; my bowels are filled with mercy*" (3 Nephi 17:7, emphasis added).

And who can forget those merciful words, "Father, forgive them; for they know not what they do?" (Luke 23:34).

Disciples Must Be Merciful

In addition to showing a magnificent example of mercy by working out the Atonement, healing the sick and the afflicted, and forgiving the soldiers, Jesus taught that we, His followers, must likewise be merciful. He taught, "Blessed are the merciful, for they shall obtain mercy" (Matthew 5:7; 3 Nephi 12:7). And "Be ye therefore merciful, as your Father also is merciful" (Luke 6:36). Jesus' beautiful parable of the Good Samaritan ends with this moral: "Which now of these three, thinkest thou, was neighbour unto him that fell among the thieves? And he said, *He that shewed mercy on him*. Then said Jesus unto him, *Go, and do thou likewise*" (Luke 10:36–37, emphasis added).

Thus, from the scriptures, we see that God is very serious about our being merciful. In Micah, we read: "What doth the Lord require of thee, but to do justly, and to love mercy, and to walk humbly with thy God?" (Micah 6:8). When it comes to loving mercy, we need to love to give it as well as loving to receive it. James, the Lord's brother, taught: "For he shall have judgment without mercy, that hath shewed no mercy" (James 2:13). Or, in other words, if we want to receive mercy, we need to show mercy. And in the end, when it's our time to be judged, it is mercy we will want, not justice.

The Book of Mormon beautifully teaches this concept of receiving mercy for mercy in the context of the law of restoration, which is the Book of Mormon way of expressing the law of the harvest:

> O, my son, this is not the case; but the meaning of the word restoration is to bring back again evil for evil, or carnal for carnal, or devilish for devilish—good for that which is good; righteous for that which is righteous; just for that which is just; *merciful for that which is merciful.* Therefore, my son, *see that you are merciful unto your brethren*; deal justly, judge righteously, and do good continually; and if ye do all these things then shall ye receive your reward; *yea, ye shall have mercy restored unto you again*; ye shall have justice restored unto you again; ye shall have a righteous judgment restored unto you again; and ye shall have good rewarded unto you again. (Alma 41:13–14, emphasis added)

If we are merciful toward others, then God will be merciful to us. But it goes beyond that. In my experience, if we are merciful toward others, others will tend to treat us mercifully. As a general rule, people treat us the way we treat them.

Being Merciful in Our Lives

How, then, are we to be merciful in our daily lives? For one thing, we can be quick to forgive and not prone to holding grudges. We can also be quick to seek forgiveness when we are in the wrong (and, in order to promote healing, sometimes even when we're not in the wrong). Inevitably, offenses will be given and taken. We are not perfect, and so sometimes we hurt others' feelings, and sometimes people hurt our feelings.

We are merciful when we are non-judgmental, when we look for the best in people, and when we don't give up on people. We are merciful when we give people the benefit of the doubt. If we gossip about another person, we are definitely not being merciful. Gossip is by nature unflattering, so when we are gossiping, we are not giving the person the benefit of the doubt. My mother—and probably everyone's mother—has advised, "If you can't say something nice, then don't say anything at all." That is great advice for a disciple of Christ who wishes to be merciful. If we are merciful, we will say something positive or simply hold our tongues.

Since being bishop of my home ward, I've often been in a setting where someone has said something derogatory about a member of my ward. The person making the negative statement then looked at me for a reaction. My standard reaction has been: "The person of whom you speak is a member of my ward, and I am the bishop. He or she deserves to have a bishop who loves him or her, so I make it a practice not to speak ill of my ward members." That usually "puts the kibosh" on the conversation. And if a bishop doesn't speak ill of his fellow ward members, why would any of us need to speak ill of one another? When I'm released, I know I will need to maintain this practice. Not gossiping is a simple matter of kindness and mercy.

A bishop knows a lot about his ward members. I have found that the more I know about a person's situation, the easier it is for me to be understanding and merciful toward him or her. Maybe that's why God is so merciful to us—He understands everything.

In the chapter on patience, I told the story of my wife being patient with a new trainee at Walmart who incompetently attempted to mix paint. When we are patient with someone who is struggling, we are showing mercy. I'm sure all of us have people close by us who are struggling and who could use our patience and mercy.

A Counterfeit of Mercy

Now let's discuss for a moment a counterfeit of mercy. I have been guilty of this counterfeit in relation to my son who struggled with drug addiction. In the modern vernacular it is called being an enabler. It means to interject oneself into a situation to rob someone of the consequences of their sin or mistake in the name of mercy. But in case you haven't noticed, God, who is infinite in mercy, doesn't do that. He usually lets us face the earthly consequences of our sins and mistakes, though often He strengthens us so that we can effectively face the consequences.

I know from my life experience that it does not help alcoholics or drug addicts to remove the consequences of their actions. I know this because I have done it. No one can conquer alcoholism or drug addiction for another person. Only the addict can conquer the addiction, on a daily basis, with the help of the grace of God.

As a bishop and a mission president, I have seen what happens when someone attempts to remove the consequences of sin in the spirit of mercy. On too many occasions, I have had a young member or missionary come to me and say something like this: "Some time ago, I committed this very bad sin (and then they tell me what it was). I confessed to my bishop, but he just said, 'Well, don't do it again.' And I haven't done it again, but I don't feel any closure or peace. Bishop/President, I did something really bad, and all the bishop said was, 'Don't do it again.' "

Depending on the severity of the sin, I usually agree with the member, institute a probationary period, and ask him or her to refrain from taking the sacrament for a period of time and read a book about the Atonement, such as *Believing Christ*, and then discuss it with me. After the probationary period has been complied with, the person often reports that, having faced consequences for the sin, there is now a feeling of peace flowing from the repentance process. If the sin in question occurred many years in the past, I sometimes tell the person I feel that there has been enough suffering worrying about the sin over the years and that the self-discipline shown in not repeating the sin is ample evidence that repentance has occurred and forgiveness has been given.

We have a dear friend named Christine Sherwood who once said that when a person acts as an enabler (such as removing the consequences from an addict or waiving the effects of sin too easily) he puts himself between the addict or sinner and his real Savior, the Lord Jesus Christ, whose mercy has the power to heal. When we interject ourselves between the sinner and his real Savior, we take away the lessons that would have been learned and the growth that would have occurred by facing the consequences with God's grace. It is not our role to do this—and, in the end, it is not helpful.

Great Examples of Mercy

When I was a young man, I was greatly moved and inspired by the excellent example of mercy shown by Pope John Paul II. On May 13, 1981, Mehmet Ali Agca, a twenty-three-year-old Turk, shot Pope John Paul II four times with a 9-millimeter pistol from a distance of fifteen feet as the Pope rode through a gathering of twenty thousand people in St. Peter's Square. The Pope barely survived the shooting and was never in as robust health as he had been prior to the attempt on his life.

As he was recovering from his injuries, the Pope asked people to "pray for my brother Agca, whom I have sincerely forgiven."[3] In 1983, he and Agca met in the prison where Agca was being held. I can remember being amazed as I saw the photographs of Pope John Paul II in the cell with his would-be assassin.

Over the years, the Pope kept in touch with Agca and his family.

On separate occasions, he visited Agca's mother and brother. In February 2005, when the Pope was ill, Agca wrote him a letter wishing him well. When the Pope died, Agca's brother said their entire family were grieving and that the Pope had been a great friend to them. Pope John Paul II was a true servant of the Lord Jesus Christ; he followed the Lord's example of mercy and, in so doing, set a marvelous example for all of us.

The Prophet Joseph Smith showed great mercy in the case of William W. Phelps, his friend and close associate who turned against him in the Missouri period, causing the Prophet substantial persecution. Joseph had previously taught that we ought to "ever keep in exercise the principle of mercy and be ready to forgive our brother on the first intimations of repentance, and asking for forgiveness; and should we even forgive our brother, or even our enemy, before he repent or ask for forgiveness, our heavenly Father would be equally merciful to us."[4]

In responding to Phelps's letter begging for forgiveness, Joseph noted that "inasmuch as long-suffering, patience, and mercy have ever characterized the dealings of our heavenly Father towards the humble and penitent, I feel disposed to copy the example, cherish the same principles, and by so doing be savior of my fellow men."[5] Joseph continued:

> It is true, that we have suffered much in consequence of your behavior—the cup of gall, already full enough for mortals to drink, was indeed filled to overflowing when you turned against us—one with whom we had oft taken sweet counsel together, and enjoyed many refreshing seasons from the Lord—had it been an enemy, we could have borne it.
>
> However, the cup has been drunk, the will of our Father has been done, and we are yet alive, for which we thank the Lord. And having been delivered from the hands of wicked men by the mercy of our God, we say it is your privilege to be delivered from the powers of the adversary, be brought into the liberty of God's dear children, and again take your stand among the saints of the Most High, and by diligence, humility, and love unfeigned, commend yourself to our God, and your God, and to the church of Jesus Christ.
>
> Believing your confession to be real, and your repentance genuine, I shall be happy once again to give you the right hand of fellowship, and rejoice over the returning prodigal.—
>
> "Come on, dear brother, since the war is past,
> "For friends at first, are friends again at last."[6]

I love that Joseph said he felt "disposed to copy the example" of Heavenly Father, who always shows mercy to the penitent. Oh, that we would all feel disposed to copy Heavenly Father's merciful example—and the examples of the Prophet Joseph Smith and Pope John Paul II!

Conclusion

God is "merciful and kind forever" (Moses 7:30). His mercy is "infinite" (Mosiah 28:4). He is "rich in mercy" (Ephesians 2:4). He has "abundant mercy" (1 Peter 1:3). The Lord is merciful to "all who will, in the sincerity of their hearts, call upon his holy name" (Helaman 3:27). He is "merciful unto those who confess their sins with humble hearts" (D&C 61:2). He is "merciful and gracious unto those who fear Him" (D&C 76:5). To those who humble themselves, cry mightily unto Him, and put their trust in Him, He will "[extend] the arm of mercy" (Mosiah 29:20). Graciously, He is "merciful unto [our] weakness" (D&C 38:14).

Mercy is one of the "weightier matters of the law" (Matthew 23:23). We will be blessed, and we will bless the lives of others, as we develop and demonstrate this Godlike attribute in our lives.

Summary

- God is very, very merciful. I counted 188 scriptural verses that mention the mercy of God or Jesus.
- Enoch was surprised when he saw God weep. God wept because He loves His children and they rejected Him, did not keep His commandments, and failed to love one another. He wept because He is full of kindness and mercy.
- God is full of mercy for all His children, but especially for those who believe on His name, love Him, and strive to keep His commandments.
- It was for mercy's sake—or in other words to make forgiveness possible—that Jesus condescended from His throne on high to come to the earth. It was for mercy's sake that He healed the sick and forgave the soldiers who participated in His crucifixion.
- The plan of salvation is called the "merciful plan of the great Creator."
- Blessed are the merciful, for they shall obtain mercy. Disciples

must give mercy if they expect to receive mercy.

- The Book of Mormon teaches that if we are merciful, we will have mercy restored to us. But it goes beyond that. In my experience, if we are merciful toward others, others will tend to be merciful in their treatment of us. As a general rule, people treat us the way we treat them.
- We can be merciful in our daily lives by being quick to forgive and not holding grudges, by seeking forgiveness when we are wrong, by being non-judgmental, by looking for the best in others, by not giving up on people, and by giving people the benefit of the doubt.
- Gossiping is the opposite of being merciful. If we can't say something nice, maybe we shouldn't say anything at all—just like our mothers taught us.
- The more we know about a person's situation, the easier it is for us to be understanding and merciful toward him or her. Maybe that's why God is so merciful to us—He understands everything.
- When we are patient with others, we are showing mercy to them.
- True mercy is not being an enabler. When we remove the consequences of others' actions, we are not showing mercy; we are actually harming them by placing ourselves between them and their real Savior.
- Pope John Paul II and the Prophet Joseph Smith showed us magnificent examples of mercy when they forgave their would-be assassin and their betrayer, respectively.
- Mercy is one of the weightier matters of the law.

Notes

1. Gordon B. Hinckley, "Blessed Are the Merciful," *Ensign*, May 1990, 68.
2. Cannon, *Gospel Truth*, vol. 1, 168.
3. Pope John Paul II, http://en.wikipedia.org/wiki/Mehmet_Ali_A%C4%9Fca
3. Joseph Smith, *History of The Church of Jesus Christ of Latter-day Saints*, vol. 3, 383.
4. Ibid., vol. 4, 163.
5. Ibid., vol. 4, 163–64.

14

Gratitude

Gratitude is a mark of a noble soul and a refined character. We like to be around those who are grateful. They tend to brighten all around them. They make others feel better about themselves.

—Joseph B. Wirthlin[1]

WHEN OUR SON TODD WAS just three years old, his mother gave him something and he immediately said, "Thanks, I appreciate that!" We thought it was so cute—and it was. But it was also a good start to his development of the important attribute of gratitude.

I have failed to find a scripture that says God the Father is grateful. That is probably because it is we who should be grateful to Him. For some reason, though, I feel that He is grateful (or at least "well pleased") when His children hearken to His words, love one another, and strive to keep His commandments. But I know for certain that His Son, Jesus Christ, was grateful; He offered thanks many times. Gratitude, therefore, is a Christlike attribute and one that we as His followers must make a part of our characters.

JESUS EXPRESSED THANKS

Jesus and his disciples ate bread "after . . . the Lord had given thanks" (John 6:23). Jesus gave thanks as He blessed the loaves and fishes with which He fed the multitudes (see Matthew 15:36; John 6:11). As Jesus was preparing to raise Lazarus from the dead, He said, "Father, I thank thee that thou hast heard me" (John 11:41). He also gave thanks as He prayed at the Last Supper: "And he took bread, and gave thanks, and brake it, and gave unto them, saying, This is my body which is given for you: this do in remembrance of me" (Luke 22:19). "And he took the cup, and gave thanks, and said, Take this, and divide it among yourselves." (Luke 22:17; and see Matthew 26:27; Mark 14:23)

After His resurrection, when He prayed to His Father on the American continent, Jesus thanked the Father that He had given the Holy Ghost to those whom He had chosen and that He had purified them (3 Nephi 19:20, 28).

Alma 7:23 is a beautiful verse that contains a listing of many divine virtues, including gratitude, "And now I would that ye should be humble, and be submissive and gentle; easy to be entreated; full of patience and long-suffering; being temperate in all things; being diligent in keeping the commandments of God at all times; asking for whatsoever things ye stand in need, both spiritual and temporal; *always returning thanks unto God for whatsoever things ye do receive*" (Alma 7:23, emphasis added).

We Should Be Grateful

We have been commanded to "thank the Lord thy God in all things" (D&C 59:7) and to "live in thanksgiving daily" (Alma 34:38). And, we have been warned that "in nothing doth man offend God, or against none is his wrath kindled, save those who confess not his hand in all things [in other words, those who are not thankful], and obey not his commandments" (D&C 59:21.) Being grateful to God, therefore, is more than a social courtesy; it is a binding commandment.

One of the evils of our time is taking for granted so many of the things we enjoy. The Lord said: "For what doth it profit a man if a gift is bestowed upon him, and he receive not the gift?" (D&C 88:33). The Apostle Paul described our day to Timothy when he wrote that in the last days "men shall be lovers of their own selves, covetous, boasters, proud, blasphemers, disobedient to parents, *unthankful*, unholy" (2 Timothy 3:2, emphasis added). These sins are linked, and ingratitude makes us susceptible to all of them.

Ingratitude is an age-old problem. You will recall that the Savior healed ten lepers, but only one returned to give thanks. Disappointed, the Savior asked, "Were there not ten cleansed? but where are the nine?" (Luke 17:17). Although not even remotely comparable to healing leprosy, Janet and I have given money or gifts to the graduating seniors in our ward for a number of years. It is the rare exception for us to receive a thank you note or even a verbal expression of thanks. When we were new in Korea, we noticed that the members and investigators often did kind acts for the missionaries. We thus took the opportunity to teach our missionaries the importance of a thank-you note. Our missionaries, ever anxious to do what their president asked, caught the vision and became adept at expressing their gratitude for the many kindnesses shown them by the Korean members, investigators, and even total strangers. I hope that habit of being grateful and expressing that gratitude has carried over into their post-mission lives.

Sometimes we have the chance to teach the expression of gratitude as we did to our missionaries, but in the end, we cannot cause others to be grateful. However, with God's help, we can make gratitude one of our personal strong points (see Ether 12:27).

Gratitude Promotes Humility

It has been said that "a proud man is seldom a grateful man." I am sure this is right. The more grateful we are, the humbler we are. The Book of Mormon and Doctrine and Covenants are filled with warnings that we must humble ourselves. And we know that the sacrifice the Lord seeks from us is a broken heart and a contrite spirit (in essence, humility). What a great thing to know that by becoming more grateful, we will also become more humble!

How to Become More Grateful

How do we become more grateful? First, we can focus our prayers on expressing thanks instead of asking for blessings and favors. In connection therewith, we can sometimes fast simply to express thanks, rather than to seek blessings. As President Joseph F. Smith once said, "The grateful man sees so much in the world to be thankful for, and with him the good outweighs the evil. Love overpowers jealousy, and light drives darkness out of his life. Pride destroys our gratitude and sets up selfishness in its place. How much happier we are in the presence of a grateful and loving soul, and how careful we should be to cultivate, through the medium of a prayerful life, a thankful attitude toward God and man!"[2]

Second, we can strive to appreciate what we have. The line, "Count your many blessings name them one by one" is not only a line from a hymn; it is also a very good idea. Periodically, we should list the many things for which we are thankful. In the best-selling book *Simple Abundance*,[3] Sara ban Breathnach encourages her readers to list, every day, five things for which they are grateful. My wife did this for over a year and found that she could take joy in small things and that doing this made her a much more grateful person.

Third, Benjamin Franklin recommended that wise men and women diminish their wants as a way of finding happiness. Being grateful for what we have will help us in diminishing our wants. When I was in my thirties, I worked for one of the largest software companies in the world. I was responsible for international legal matters and traveled to many countries, including China, India, Pakistan, Nepal, Southeast Asia, and Latin America. I learned, rather quickly, that much of the world lives in very modest conditions. My lifestyle, middle class as it was, was wealthy in comparison. My travels helped me resist the desire for a bigger house; they made me grateful for what I already had and helped me to diminish my wants for material things.

President Spencer W. Kimball aptly noted: "In many countries, the homes are barren and the cupboards are bare—no books, no radios, no pictures, no furniture, no fire—while we are housed adequately, clothed warmly, and fed extravagantly. Did we show our thanks by the proper devotion on our knees last night and this morning and tomorrow? Ingratitude, thou sinful habit!"[4]

Fourth, we can resist the tendency to compare ourselves with others. I love this example from the life of Andrew Lindsay, who is about to graduate from Timpanogos High School. Andrew has served faithfully and effectively as my first assistant in the priest quorum of our ward. His father is a stake president at BYU, and his mother sings with the Tabernacle Choir. When Andrew was young, he was thrilled by the concept of trick-or-treating. You just dress up in a costume and all the nice people in the neighborhood give you candy for no apparent reason. Little Andrew beamed with happiness that first memorable

Halloween night as he returned home and dumped out the precious contents of his little pumpkin-shaped bucket. He could not have been happier—until, that is, his older brothers returned home with their pillowcases full of candy and dumped them out on the floor beside his pile. His older brothers' piles dwarfed his little pile of candy from his small pumpkin container. Joy instantly turned to sorrow as Andrew compared his meager take with the massive candy piles of his older brothers, and Andrew began to cry.

It was comparing that took Andrew from ecstasy to agony in a matter of seconds. Andrew is grown now, but we all can benefit from his experience. There will always be someone who has more than we do—someone with a larger house, someone with a better car, someone with more money, someone who is better looking, someone who is smarter, someone who is better off in some way than we are. Recently I had lunch with a man who has a bit of American Indian blood flowing in his veins. For many years he has received a tax-free monthly check of $20,000 from a resort his tribe runs in California. For a brief second, I caught myself thinking longingly of what my life would be like if I had $20,000 a month coming in without having to do anything for it. Then I came back to my reality. Somehow we need to develop the discipline to count our own many blessings without comparing them to the blessings of others.

It is clear from the above discussion that unbridled materialism is not consistent with the development of gratitude. The more materialistic we are, the less likely we are to be satisfied with our situation. The Apostle Paul said, "Not that I speak in respect of want: for I have learned, in whatsoever state I am, therewith to be content" (Philippians 4:11). He also wisely taught: "But godliness with contentment is great gain. For we brought nothing into this world, and it is certain we can carry nothing out. And having food and raiment let us be therewith content" (1 Timothy 6:6–8). Paul, like many of the Lord's anointed, was not "blessed" (or "cursed," depending on how you look at it) with wealth. Similarly, when Peter and John encountered the lame man at the gate of the temple, Peter said, "Silver and gold have I none; but such as I have give I thee" (Acts 3:6). And then he healed the man with his priesthood power.

Scriptures too numerous to quote teach us to give thanks unto God. One says, "It is a good thing to give thanks unto the Lord" (Psalm

92:1). Daniel gave thanks in his prayers three times a day (see Daniel 6:10). We should thank the Lord every day (see Mosiah 18:23), morning and evening (see 1 Chronicles 23:30; Alma 37:37), by day and by night (see 2 Nephi 9:52), and all the day long (Ether 6:9). It is the will of God that we give thanks in all things and in everything (see 1 Thessalonians 5:18; Mosiah 26:39; D&C 62:7; D&C 78:19; D&C 98:1).

We are to thank God for his mercy (Psalm 136:1) and holiness (Psalm 30:4). Importantly, we should give thanks to God who has given us the "victory through our Lord Jesus Christ" (1 Corinthians 15:57) and who has caused us to "triumph in Christ" (2 Corinthians 2:14).

We have so much for which to be thankful—life itself; the Atonement; our knowledge of the purpose of life; the Restoration of the gospel; our family members and friends; our material possessions; our freedom; the influence of the Holy Ghost; the opportunity to serve in our Church callings; and much, much more.

Conclusion

When I was serving as mission president, I was asked without prior warning to speak briefly to a group of new converts. The fact that I had to speak in Korean made it doubly difficult, but my first instinct was to tell them how thankful I was for my membership in The Church of Jesus Christ of Latter-day Saints. Following is the gist of what I said on that occasion.

I still remember my baptism day clearly, even though it was forty years ago. I was baptized on September 10, 1961. It was a beautiful, bright, clear, late-summer day. I was eight years old. I had a simple understanding of the gospel, but I knew the importance of baptism, and I felt the spirit strongly on my baptism day.

My membership in the Church has been a continuing blessing in my life. Here, briefly, is why I am grateful to be a member of The Church of Jesus Christ of Latter-day Saints:

- I know the nature of God.
- And because I know the nature of God, I know who I am—a son of God with divine potential. So I know what my destiny can be.
- The plan of salvation, also called the plan of happiness, gives

me hope. I know that I will see my deceased parents, whom I dearly love, again.

- The gospel gives me an eternal perspective that helps me avoid mistakes.
- Eternal marriage and the sealing power give me hope. Love is eternal. People die, but love does not.
- I know of the Atonement and its power of salvation and its enabling power.
- I have fellowship with members of this Church who are among the best people in the world.

We can "live in thanksgiving daily" (Alma 34:38). It all starts with a prayer of gratitude in the morning and a prayer of thankfulness at night. Gratitude is indeed the "mark of a noble soul and a refined character."[5]

SUMMARY

- Jesus often expressed thanks in His prayers to His Father in Heaven.
- We are to thank the Lord in all things and to live in thanksgiving daily. Being grateful to God is a commandment.
- Ingratitude is one of the evils of our time, yet it is an age-old problem as well. Jesus healed ten lepers, but only one returned to give thanks.
- We cannot cause others to be grateful. But, with God's help, we can make gratitude one of our personal strong points.
- A proud man is seldom a grateful man. Being grateful helps us become humble.
- We can become more grateful by:

    1. Focusing our prayers on expressing gratitude, rather than asking for things
    2. Fasting to express thanks
    3. Striving to appreciate what we have by counting our many blessings
    4. Diminishing our wants
    5. Resisting the tendency to compare ourselves with others
    6. Avoiding materialism

- We should give thanks to the Lord always, in everything.
- We have much to be thankful for, including the many blessings of Church membership.
- Thankfulness starts with a prayer of thanksgiving each morning and with a prayer of gratitude each evening.

Notes

1. Joseph B. Wirthlin, "Live in Thanksgiving Daily," *Ensign*, Sept. 2001, 8.
2. Joseph F. Smith, *Gospel Doctrine: Selections from the Sermons and Writings of Joseph F. Smith*, comp. John A. Widtsoe (Salt Lake City: Deseret Book, 1939), 263.
3. Sarah ban Breathnach, *Simple Abundance* (New York: Warner Books, 1995), entry for January 14.
4. Spencer W. Kimball, *Teachings of Spencer W. Kimball*, 252.
5. Wirthlin, "Live in Thanksgiving Daily," 8.

15

Happiness

LDS doctrine teaches that joy is obtained only by righteousness. Consequently, Latter-day Saints view God's commandments as loving counsel from a wise Father—a Father whose goal is human happiness. They believe that lives which conform to God's will and are governed by his standards will create the most joyful response to all of life's circumstances, bringing both a fulfillment in life's accomplishments and a sweet resolve in life's sorrows.

—*Encyclopedia of Mormonism*[1]

If you were to ask 100 percent of the people in the world what they most want, I am sure that over 90 percent of them would answer, "I want to be happy." Happiness and joy are the topic of this chapter. Happiness is one of the divine virtues. President Heber C. Kimball said: "I am perfectly satisfied that my Father and my God is a cheerful, pleasant, lively, good-natured Being. Why? Because I am cheerful, pleasant, lively, and good-natured when I have His Spirit. That is one reason why I know; and another is—the Lord said, through Joseph Smith, 'I delight in a glad heart and a cheerful countenance.' That arises from the perfection of His attributes; He is a jovial, lively person, and a beautiful man."[2]

God Is a Happy Being

God is a happy Being, and it is our ultimate goal to become like Him. So we cannot be like Him if we are not happy. When we have His Spirit with us, we will be happy—as well as cheerful, pleasant, lively, and good-natured. In fact, the purpose of the Atonement is to permit us to live in a state of never-ending happiness. "And he hath brought to pass the redemption of the world, whereby he that is found guiltless before him at the judgment day hath it given unto him to dwell in the presence of God in his kingdom, to sing ceaseless praises with the choirs above, unto the Father, and unto the Son, and unto the Holy Ghost, which are one God, *in a state of happiness which hath no end*" (Mormon 7:7, emphasis added).

In this world, though, how and in what ways do people seek happiness? Here are just some of the ways:

- Power
- Fame
- Wealth
- Sex
- Travel
- Acquiring goods
- Love
- Children
- Alcohol and drugs
- High positions at work or church

Happiness Is the Object and Design of Our Existence

The Prophet Joseph taught, "Happiness is the object and design of our existence; and will be the end thereof, if we pursue the path that leads to it; and this path is virtue, uprightness, faithfulness, holiness, and keeping all the commandments of God."[3]

So, happiness is actually the purpose of our existence and the reason we are here on the earth. We find happiness through keeping the commandments of God. The scriptures support Joseph's teaching on this subject. We learn from the Book of Mormon that "Adam fell that men might be; and men are, that they might have joy" (2 Nephi 2:25). The Book of Mormon also calls the plan of salvation "the great plan of happiness" (Alma 42:8).

In fact, the scriptures describe the things that bring happiness and joy.

- Following righteousness (Abraham 1:2)
- Repentance and humility (Alma 27:17–18)
- Correction by God (Job 5:17)
- Children (Psalm 127:3–5; 3 John 1:4)
- Recognizing the Lord (Psalm 144:15; 146:5)
- Helping the poor (Proverbs 14:21)
- Keeping the commandments (Proverbs 29:18; Mosiah 2:41)
- Serving one another (John 13:13–17)
- Enduring (James 5:11)
- Suffering for righteousness' sake (1 Peter 3:14; 1 Peter 4:14; 2 Nephi 9:18)
- Dying in the faith (Alma 46:41)
- The Holy Ghost (D&C 11:13; Acts 13:52; Romans 14:17; Galatians 5:22–23; Alma 22:15)
- The remission of sins (Mosiah 4:3; Alma 36:20–21)
- Resurrection (Alma 4:14; see D&C 93:33–34)
- Sharing the gospel (D&C 18:15–16)
- Mysteries and peaceable things (D&C 42:61)
- The gospel (glad tidings of great joy) (D&C 79:1)

Obedience and the Holy Spirit

Based on the number of scriptural references I found, the two things most likely to bring happiness are keeping the commandments (see Mosiah 2:41) and enjoying the influence of the Holy Ghost (see D&C 11:13). In my opinion the two scriptures cited immediately below are the best in making this point:

Obeying the Commandments

"And moreover, I would desire that ye should consider on *the blessed and happy state of those that keep the commandments of God*. For behold, they are blessed in all things, both temporal and spiritual; and if they hold out faithful to the end they are received into heaven, that thereby they may dwell with God *in a state of never-ending happiness*. O remember, remember that these things are true; for the Lord God hath spoken it" (Mosiah 2:41, emphasis added).

The Holy Ghost (or the Spirit)

"Verily, verily, I say unto you, I will impart unto you of *my Spirit, which shall* enlighten your mind, which shall *fill your soul with joy*" (D&C 11:13, emphasis added).

There it is: joy comes from obedience. It is a gift of the Spirit and comes from the Holy Ghost. To summarize:

Obedience → Spirit → Happiness

Obedience leads to having the Spirit, which leads to happiness. That's the formula. The early disciples "were filled with joy, and with the Holy Ghost" (Acts 13:52). The kingdom of God is "righteousness, and peace, and joy in the Holy Ghost" (Romans 14:17). And the "fruit of the Spirit" includes "joy" (Galatians 5:22).

FINDING HAPPINESS

So how does this work? How could our pioneer ancestors be happy in the midst of the most intense persecution? President George Q. Cannon provides the answer:

> I have spoken about the afflictions, trials, and persecutions that we have had to contend with; but in the midst of all these things there is one truth that should be stated concerning the Latter-day Saints, and that is, that they are the happiest people, with all these difficulties, that ever lived upon the face of the earth. I do not believe that such a people can be found anywhere. I do not believe that there is so much happiness enjoyed by any community, however favorably constituted, however many the advantages which it may possess, as by these Latter-day Saints. The reason of this is that when they go to the Lord, if they are in trouble, if they are perplexed, if they do not know what to do, He hears and answers their prayers, and gives unto them glad hearts. They ought always to have cheerful countenances; they ought to be an exceedingly happy people; and I believe they are. We have every reason to be thankful. Where can you travel on the face of the earth and see such union and such love exhibited and enjoyed as you find amongst this people?[4]

My experience, too, is that Latter-day Saints are the happiest people on the earth. One of our great missionaries in the Korea Daejeon Mission, Elder Sean Stewart, shared a profound thought in his testimony in zone leader council one day. He said, "I have visited a lot of less-active members on my mission, but I have never met a less-active member who was as happy as an active one."

The great Jewish psychologist Viktor Frankl taught that we can choose our attitude. In a sense, we can choose happiness. We know from the scriptures that wickedness never was happiness (see Alma 41:10), but it is also true that righteousness is not always happiness. We will have trials in this world. There will be sad days and weeks and months. But, through it all, we can have peace through the gospel—and we can have happiness most of the time, even in this life.

Be of Good Cheer

Speaking of attitude, let us consider the teachings of our Lord Jesus Christ, who often encouraged His followers to be of good cheer. "And, behold, they brought to him a man sick of the palsy, lying on a bed: and Jesus seeing their faith said unto the sick of the palsy; Son, be of good cheer; thy sins be forgiven thee" (Matthew 9:2). On another occasion, "straightway Jesus spake unto them, saying, Be of good cheer; it is I; be not afraid" (Matthew 14:27). He also said, "These things I have spoken unto you, that in me ye might have peace. In the world ye shall have tribulation: but be of good cheer; I have overcome the world" (John 16:33).

In Acts we read, "And the night following the Lord stood by him, and said, Be of good cheer, Paul: for as thou hast testified of me in Jerusalem, so must thou bear witness also at Rome" (Acts 23:11). The Book of Mormon tells us, "Lift up your head and be of good cheer; for behold, the time is at hand, and on this night shall the sign be given, and on the morrow come I into the world, to show unto the world that I will fulfil all that which I have caused to be spoken by the mouth of my holy prophets" (3 Nephi 1:13).

Consider this passage from the Doctrine and Covenants: "And now, verily I say unto you, and what I say unto one I say unto all, be of good cheer, little children; for I am in your midst, and I have not forsaken you" (D&C 61:36). And this one: "Wherefore, be of good cheer, and do not fear, for I the Lord am with you, and will stand by you; and ye shall bear record of me, even Jesus Christ, that I am the Son of the living God, that I was, that I am, and that I am to come" (D&C 68:6).

Jesus also said, "And ye cannot bear all things now; nevertheless, be of good cheer, for I will lead you along. The kingdom is yours and the blessings thereof are yours, and the riches of eternity are yours" (D&C 78:18). Finally, He said, "Let thy heart be of good cheer before my face; and thou shalt bear record of my name, not only unto the Gentiles, but also unto the Jews; and thou shalt send forth my word unto the ends of the earth" (D&C 112:4). I think Jesus is serious about our being cheerful, positive, upbeat, and hopeful.

Who do you know who seems to be happy and cheerful? Our former prophet, President Hinckley, is one person who comes to mind. He always seemed to be happy and of good cheer. He had a quick sense of humor. He knew more about what was wrong with in world and the Church than anyone else, but he chose to be positive and to look on the bright side. In his words, he chose to "accentuate the positive."

Although he suffered constantly at the hands of his enemies, the Prophet Joseph, with his "native cheery temperament," was another wonderful example of being happy and cheerful.

When we served our mission in Korea, many of our young missionaries were perpetually cheerful and happy, no matter the situation. If they were serving in the strongest ward in a metropolitan area like Gwangju, they were happy to be there. When I transferred them to the countryside to help with a fledging branch, they could not have been happier about the challenge. If I gave them a struggling companion and asked them to mentor their companion, they cheerfully did so. There were certain missionaries who made a major impact for good on every ward or branch in which they served—so much so that when transfer time was approaching, I would receive a panicked call from the bishop or branch president begging me not to transfer that elder or sister. (I transferred them anyway, if it was their time to go.) These wonderful elders and sisters chose to be happy and cheerful. Because of their attitude and diligence, they were "impact players," strongly influencing for good every ward, branch, companion, member, less-active member, investigator, or total stranger who came within their sphere.

Think of someone you know who seems to be perpetually happy, who faces challenges, problems, and sorrows with cheerfulness and hope. It could be your mother or father, a sibling, a neighbor, a close friend, a Church leader, or a teacher. What makes them tick? Why are they so happy? Why do they have a "glad heart and a cheerful countenance?"

(D&C 59:15). Some people, even if they are not particularly good people, have a "native cheery temperament." But in the gospel context, what makes us happy and cheerful is righteousness—striving to keep the commandments and, as a result, enjoying the influence of the Holy Spirit. The gospel of the Lord Jesus Christ is itself the "good tidings of great joy, which shall be to all people" (Luke 2:10; see D&C 79:1).

Ammon in the Book of Mormon was "swallowed up in the joy of his God," a "joy which none receiveth save it be the truly penitent and humble seeker of happiness" (Alma 27:17–18). Like Ammon, we too will be "filled with joy" when we receive a "remission of our sins" (Mosiah 4:3). The early Nephites, during a period of righteousness, "lived after the manner of happiness"(2 Nephi 5:27). The repentant Alma reported that there was "nothing so exquisite and sweet as was [his] joy" (Alma 36:21). In fact, it is "contrary to the nature of that righteousness which is in our great and Eternal Head" to find "happiness in doing iniquity" (Helaman 13:38).

Happiness or Peace at Times of Suffering

But isn't it true that sometimes the righteous suffer? The Apostle Peter taught that those who "suffer for righteousness' sake" and those who are "reproached for the name of Christ" will be happy (1 Peter 3:14; 1 Peter 4:14). How is it possible to be happy while suffering for the Lord's sake? The people of Alma found that "the Lord provided for them that they should hunger not, neither should they thirst; yea, and he also gave them strength, that they should suffer no manner of afflictions, save it were swallowed up in the joy of Christ" (Alma 31:38). In the end, "the righteous, the saints of the Holy One of Israel, they who have believed in the Holy One of Israel, they who have endured the crosses of the world, and despised the shame of it, they shall inherit the kingdom of God, which was prepared for them from the foundation of the world, and *their joy shall be full forever*" (2 Nephi 9:18, emphasis added).

It is a fact that we can only receive a fulness of joy in a resurrected, exalted state (D&C 93:33–34). However, we can experience much joy and happiness as we wend our way through this mortal life. BYU professor Rodney Turner said, "God is in the business of 'happifying' his children by sharing his own nature with them. A perpetually unhappy

Saint is an oxymoron, a self-contradiction. Consequently, when all is said and done, each of us will be as happy as we have chosen to be, which is to say, we will be as much one with God as we have chosen to be."[5]

Life is hard. There are tests and trials. Yet, we must make the effort to be cheerful and to be happy. God's Spirit is a "happifying" spirit. Because of trials and tribulations, it may be hard to be happy for a time, but for the righteous, there will be peace. And this peace will come because of our faith in the Lord. "And it came to pass that there came a voice unto them, yea, a pleasant voice, as if it were a whisper, saying: Peace, peace be unto you, because of your faith in my Well Beloved, who was from the foundation of the world" (Helaman 5:46–47).

When we presided over the Korea Daejeon Mission, a wonderful couple named Rob and Robin Slover presided over the Korea Busan Mission. When President and Sister Slover had been on their mission for about five months, their college-aged son died unexpectedly because of a bad reaction to prescription medicine. What a traumatic event this was in the Slover family—as it would be in any family. Sister Slover received permission to return to the United States, to make all the necessary arrangements, and to attend the funeral services. However, President Slover had to remain at his post to take care of his missionaries. In his farewell testimony at the North Asia Area Mission President Seminar two and a half years later President Slover said, "One of the names given to the Holy Ghost is the Comforter. I know from poignant personal experience that the Holy Ghost is just that—he really is the Comforter, and he really does comfort." When President Slover said these words, everyone in the room knew what he was referring to, and there was not a dry eye in the house. I was deeply touched by President Slover's testimony. During his time of intense sorrow, there was no happiness, but there were comfort and peace.

Joy Is the Pathway to Celestial Glory

One of the happiest, most jovial souls of all was Elder Matthew Cowley, a former member of the Quorum of the Twelve Apostles. Elder Cowley said, "I think sometimes we can take ourselves too seriously, and sometimes when we do take ourselves too seriously, especially as teachers, I'm afraid those whom we are endeavoring to teach get the impression that we are trying to frighten them into the celestial glory. Don't ever try to frighten anyone into the celestial glory. Joy is the pathway to the celestial glory—joy and happiness. We must lead with love and charity and happiness those with whom we are working to get them into the celestial glory."[6] I agree with Elder Cowley wholeheartedly.

One of the nicest compliments I ever received came from President Sol Yang Hwan, the Daejeon stake president, at a farewell fireside just before we completed our service in Korea and returned to the United States. I was deeply touched when, at the beginning of the meeting, President Sol said,

> It's hard sometimes for us in Korea to be faithful latter-day saints. We have so many "don'ts" and so many "do's." Sometimes we are so discouraged and so serious. And then along comes President Rife. He is laughing and joking and cheerful. He tells us that our God is a happy God and that we should be happy too. He shows us that living the gospel can be fun. When I see President Rife, I think of the following scripture from the New Testament which describes him: "Rejoice in the Lord alway: and again I say, Rejoice" (Philippians 4:4).

Interestingly, the Korean New Testament does not use the word *rejoice*; rather, it uses the phrase "be happy." So, as President Sol read the scripture, it was: "Be happy in the Lord always; and again I say, be happy." I know that we can "be happy in the Lord." There really is no other way we can be truly happy.

Conclusion

Everyone wants to be happy. The world seeks happiness largely through artificial means. However, we know the right way to seek happiness. It comes as a gift of the Spirit through keeping the commandments of God. Obedience brings the Spirit, which brings joy and happiness. May we always "consider on the blessed and happy state of those that keep the commandments of God" (Mosiah 2:41).

Summary

- All people want to be happy. Happiness is one of the Godlike attributes, for our God is a cheerful, pleasant, lively, and good-natured Being.

- If we have God's Spirit to be with us, we will be happy. It is a purpose of the Atonement to permit us to live in a state of never-ending happiness.
- In the world, many people seek happiness through false and artificial means.
- Happiness is the object and design of our existence and will be the end thereof if we keep the commandments of God. Men are that they might have joy. The plan of salvation is called the "great plan of happiness."
- The scriptures teach many things that bring happiness and joy, including obedience and the Spirit of God. Joy comes from obedience; it is a gift of the Spirit and comes from the Holy Ghost. Obedience leads to having the Spirit, which leads to happiness.
- Latter-day Saints are, and should be, among the happiest people on the earth.
- We can choose our attitude; we can choose happiness. Wickedness never was happiness, but righteousness is not always happiness.
- Jesus often encouraged His followers to be of good cheer.
- We have many examples of people who have followed Jesus' counsel and who are persons of good cheer. These people are righteous and thus enjoy the influence of the Holy Spirit, which brings joy and peace.
- Joy comes to the truly penitent and humble seeker of happiness.
- It is contrary to the nature of God to find ultimate happiness in doing iniquity.
- Saints who suffer for righteousness' sake will be happy—they may have their suffering of afflictions "swallowed up in the joy of Christ."
- We can only receive a fulness of joy in a resurrected, exalted state.
- Still, we can have much joy and happiness in this life. A perpetually unhappy saint is an oxymoron, a self-contradiction. Even when happiness cannot be found, a saint can experience peace through faith in the Lord.

Notes

1. *Encyclopedia of Mormonism*, 771.

2. Heber C. Kimball in *Journal of Discourses*, vol. 4 (London: Latter-day Saints' Book Depot, 1854), 222.
3. Joseph Smith, *Teachings of the Prophet Joseph Smith*, 255.
4. George Q. Cannon in *Collected Discourses 1886–1898*, vol. 1 (Salt Lake City: Deseret Book, 2009). Originally dated February 24, 1889.
5. Rodney Turner, *The Lectures on Faith in Historical Perspective*, ed. Larry E. Dahl and Charles D. Tate Jr. (Provo: BYU Religious Studies Center, 1990), 218.
6. Matthew Cowley, *Matthew Cowley Speaks* (Salt Lake City: Deseret Book, 1954), 132–33.

16

Conclusion

Life is an aspiration. Its mission is to strive after perfection, which is self-realization. The ideal must not be lowered because of our weaknesses or imperfections. I am painfully conscious of both in me. The silent cry daily goes out to Truth to help me to remove these weaknesses and imperfections of mine.

—Mahatma Gandhi[1]

While writing this book, I attended the Draper Utah Temple dedication broadcast in my stake center. As I was waiting for the dedication service to begin, I thought about the effort and expense we make as a people to build temples. When we build a temple, which is the house of the Lord, we go all out. Nothing is too good for the Lord. The buildings are exquisitely constructed. They have beautiful molding and murals, windows and chandeliers. When completed, we present the beautiful building to the Lord.

If we are that careful in constructing a building, shouldn't we put the same—or even greater—care into the building of our characters? God's work and glory is not the building of temples; it is the immortality and eternal life of man (see Moses 1:39), the building of souls. Temple building, while sacred and holy, is just a means to an end—and the end is our eternal lives, as God's sons and daughters.

That's what this book has been about—building a character that will lead to eternal life. We have discussed in some detail the interrelated divine virtues outlined in the scriptures:

- Humility and meekness
- Obedience and submissiveness
- Faith and hope
- Charity and love
- Patience and long-suffering
- Temperance
- Diligence
- Kindness and gentleness
- Easiness in being entreated
- Virtue, holiness, and godliness
- Knowledge
- Mercy
- Gratitude
- Happiness

We have noted that while perfection is not expected of us in this life, it is possible to become a very Christlike individual. Such persons exist in the scriptures, but we all know people with whom we have interacted that are far along the pathway to perfection. Over time, with the help of God, these persons have, in large measure, developed the divine virtues in their lives.

As you look again at the qualities listed above, please think, "Which ones seem to be a part of my character, either because I am naturally that way (it's my spiritual gift) or because I have already worked to develop them? Have others praised me for possessing any of the other qualities?" If so, then it is likely that that quality is one of your strong points. After you have analyzed the qualities you possess, ask yourself "Which ones are my weaknesses?"

I am sure that as you go through this exercise, you will inherently know which qualities are your strong points and which ones are your weak points. Pick a divine virtue that is a weak point for you and that you feel impressed to work on. Read again about that attribute. Think about it. And, as Aristotle advised, practice it. Remember that Aristotle taught that men acquire a particular quality by constantly acting a particular way. "It is by doing just acts that we become just, by doing temperate actions we become temperate, by doing courageous actions we become courageous."[2] If we practice a quality long enough, we will eventually possess that quality. Pray for it. Don't be discouraged, and don't give up. Don't run faster than you have strength. Keep at it. Focus on that attribute for a month, or even a year.

Each year, my wife chooses one word that will be her theme for that year. One year she chose the word *simplicity*. In every decision she made, in everything she did, she asked the question, "Will this help me create a simple life?" (We saved a lot of money that year!) The same approach can be used with the divine virtues.

Several years ago, when I went through this exercise, I selected humility as an attribute I needed to work on. Through focusing on it in the above manner—reading about it, thinking about it, practicing it, and praying for it—I feel I made some progress, although as you know, if I say I am humble then I am proud of my humility. So I keep working on it. My dear wife chose temperance and worked on it for a year. And, as you would suppose, in so doing, she became a much more temperate person. She's still working at it, though.

Remember the formula we learned earlier in the book? Based on Ether 12:27, it was:

Humility + Faith = Strength

Select the attribute you feel is your weakness. Ask the Lord in faith and humility to help you convert that weakness into a strength. Allow Him, over time, to change your heart in the ways necessary to make this possible. And, simultaneously, try to acquire this attribute yourself by your own effort and with your own focused practice.

There is no doubt that it's important, in seeking after the divine virtues, to read the scriptures and to pray for a change of heart. A daily Sacred Grove experience in the solitude of our personal sacred sites will surely help. Studying, even memorizing, the Christlike attributes will help us retain them in mind and will certainly be a benefit. But, in reality, we cannot acquire the divine nature in the quietude of our den. The divine virtues are not developed in a vacuum. They are developed while interacting with people; they're acquired, through practice, while bumping up against humanity. We learn to be kind and charitable, patient and temperate in our dealings with our spouses, children, other family members, ward members, neighbors, fellow citizens, and other drivers on the road. And so, to take upon ourselves the divine nature, we need to close the scriptures, get up from our knees, and practice these Christlike qualities as we interact with the people who cross our path and come within our sphere of influence.

After I had written the first draft of this book, my wife and I were driving to a wedding reception and the car in front of us was going ten miles per hour in a thirty-five-mile-per-hour zone. Impatiently (but without honking at least), I questioned the driver's IQ level. My wife responded by saying, "This is a chance for you to practice patience." I then said, "It's times like these that make me wish I hadn't written that book about being perfect." We laughed, but it's true that we aren't perfect, and we won't be perfect in this life. Still, we can and should be seeking to acquire these divine virtues. And, with God's enabling power, we can make great progress. I can even learn to be more patient with other drivers.

As quoted earlier, the Apostle Paul said, "But refuse profane and old wives' fables, and exercise thyself rather unto godliness. For bodily exercise profiteth little: but godliness is profitable unto all things, having promise of the life that now is, and of that which is to come" (1 Timothy 4:7–8, emphasis added). What a blessing, both now and eternally, to seek after godliness or, in other words, the divine virtues. In the long run, we will have our sins washed clean, and we will be in a position to inherit eternal life. But striving for the divine attributes will also improve our lives, here and now. I believe that people who have developed the Christlike attributes are happier as they go through life. They are at peace with God and man. They have a calmness, a deep and abiding spirituality, and an eternal perspective. There is a saying that virtue (one of the divine attributes) is its own reward. But I would contend that all the divine attributes are their own reward, both here and hereafter.

President George Q. Cannon said, "We are the children of God, and as His children there is no attribute we ascribe to Him that we do not possess, though they may be dormant or in embryo. The mission of the Gospel is to develop these powers and make us like our Heavenly Parent. I know this is true, and such knowledge makes me feel happy."[3] I add my testimony to that of President Cannon. I know this is true—and this knowledge makes me happy too.

I suppose we have all attended a meeting (such as priesthood leadership or auxiliary training) that left us feeling discouraged rather than encouraged, and chastised rather than appreciated. That is not the feeling I intended to create in this book. No doubt becoming like God is a daunting challenge, but God, whose patience and mercy are infinite, is willing to work with us, as long as we are willing to try. The quest for the divine virtues will be a long one and will, undoubtedly, extend beyond this mortal life. Thus, we need to be patient with ourselves, but we also need to be diligent and keep at it. We can make much progress, with the Lord's enabling power. God has told us, through His scriptures and through prophets like President Cannon, that we can become like our Heavenly Parents and that it is our mission to do so.

And so, as we conclude, I wish to encourage all of us in this ongoing quest for the divine nature. The Lord has said, "And that which doth not edify is not of God" (D&C 50:23). I hope that as you have read this book, you have not been discouraged, but you have been inspired, encouraged, enlightened, uplifted—and yes, edified.

I testify that God lives and that Jesus is the Christ. They are the embodiment of the divine virtues. We are created in their image. Their attributes are a part of our nature, even if merely in embryo. We can develop these attributes, and as we do so, we will find happiness and peace in this life and eternal life in the world to come. I express gratitude to the Prophet Joseph Smith through whom the Restoration was effected. Because of the Restoration we know who God is, who we are, and who we can become.

Taking upon ourselves the divine nature, as the Apostle Peter encouraged, is the great quest of our lives, the great adventure, the great journey. It is my sincere prayer that we may never give up; that we may press forward with faith; and that we may keep hope alive.

And so I close this book as I began Chapter 1, with a beautiful quote from then Elder Marion G. Romney, which sums up everything I wish to convey in this book:

> When men correctly understand and have faith in the true and living God, they strive to develop within themselves his virtues. He becomes the lodestar of their lives. To emulate him is their highest aspiration. As they strive to "be . . . perfect, even as [their] Father which is in heaven is perfect" (Matthew 5:48), they actually become partakers of his divine nature. In doing so, they add to their faith and knowledge, temperance, patience, godliness, brotherly kindness, love, and charity, virtues that are perfected in the true and

living God. These virtues drive out of their hearts selfishness, greed, lust, hate, contentions, and war. Happiness, contentment, joy, and peace naturally follow.[4]

SUMMARY

- When we build a temple, we go all out, for nothing is too good for the Lord. Should we not put the same—or even greater—effort into building our characters?
- God's work and glory is building souls. That is what this book has been about—building a character that will lead you to eternal life.
- We have studied the divine virtues one by one in this book. Perfection is not expected of us in this life, but it is possible to make great progress. It is possible to become a very Christlike individual.
- As we look at the divine virtues, some will be our strong points, others our weak points. We can select a weak point and begin to work on it. We can read about it, think about it, pray for it, and practice it.
- As we practice one virtue long enough, it becomes part of us. We needn't be discouraged when we fail. We can just keep trying.
- In developing an attribute, we can use the formula from Ether 12:27, which is Humility + Faith = Strength. We ask God for help, and He will change our hearts, gradually, over time, as we give our best effort to develop the attribute.
- As important as it is to study about the divine virtues and to pray for them, we will only develop them through practice, with God's help, as we interact with our fellow human beings.
- By attempting to take upon ourselves the divine nature, one virtue at a time, we will ultimately be in a position to receive eternal life, but we will also be happier here and now.
- "Virtue is its own reward," but in fact all the Christlike attributes are their own reward.
- We are the children of God, and there is no attribute we ascribe to Him that we do not possess, albeit in embryo.
- Trying to become like God is a daunting challenge, but God (whose mercy and patience are infinite) will work with us as long as we keep trying. We need to be patient with ourselves while also

being diligent. We needn't be discouraged. We can become like our Heavenly Parents.

- This book was not written to discourage, but rather to inspire, encourage, uplift, and edify.
- Taking upon ourselves the divine nature, as the Apostle Peter encouraged, is the great quest of our lives, the great adventure, the great journey.
- As we emulate our Father in Heaven and His Son Jesus Christ, we gradually take upon ourselves the divine virtues. This process drives out selfishness, greed, lust, hate, contentions, and war. Happiness, contentment, joy, and peace naturally follow.

Notes

1. Mahatma Gandhi, *All Men Are Brothers*, ed. Krishna Kripalani (New York: Continuum, 2008), 68.
2. Aristotle, *Nicomachean Ethics*, 43.
3. Cannon, *Gospel Truth*, vol. 1, 1.
4. Romney in Conference Report, 67.

About the Author

Richard Rife has practiced international law and has served as general counsel for several large companies. He has English and law degrees from Brigham Young University and is the author of *Honoring Christmas in My Heart*.

He has served in many callings in the Church, including full-time missionary, elders quorum president, branch president, bishop, temple sealer, Gospel Doctrine teacher, and Primary pianist. He and Sister Rife presided over the Korea Daejeon Mission from 2001 to 2004. He is currently serving as bishop of his home ward.

Brother Rife and his wife, Janet, are the parents of six children and make their home in Orem, Utah. He welcomes reader comments to his email address, rrifekorea@hotmail.com, and invites readers to view his website: http://richardrife.com.

0 26575 53900 4